The Speculative Art Of Alchemy: A Textbook On The Art Of Self-Regeneration

A. S. Raleigh

TABLE OF CONTENTS

INTRODUCTORY NOTE

The sermon of Hermes "About the Common Mind," deals with the Common or General Mind as the principle or Energy radiating from the God Beyond All Name, and its relation to the individual mind in man, as well as all other forms of life, in so far as they are dominated by Mind. The position taken by Hermes is that the thinking of the Supreme Divinity is radiated forth as Mind, possessing the same essentiality as does the very Esse of God. This Mind it is that dominates all the creative life of Cosmos. All else is the product of this Mind. This is termed the Common Mind, because it is the Mind common to all. In man it becomes individualized as the mind, which becomes the energizing principle of the soul. We must never confuse it with the soul, for it is not a part of the soul, but rather an Energy entering into the soul and energizing it to act contrary to its own nature. The soul has three modes of psychic activity; the natural mode, which is the action of the soul through its own *nature,* that is, the spontaneous genesis of the soul within herself; the sensuous, or the psychic reaction of the soul to the energizing of the Psyche by the senses, particularly those of the body; and the mental, which is the action of the soul, when energized by the mind, which means the energizing of her by the Mind. This leads to three orders of life for every human soul. There is the *natural* life which she leads when she is not interferred with by the senses, the spontaneous soul life. Next we find the degenerate life of the soul which she leads when her psyche is energized by the senses of the body, resulting in the imaging of the senses or their objects in the soul, so that her functioning is determined by

these images of sensibles. Lastly, there is the Regenerate
life of the soul, which she leads when she is energized
by the action of the mind. This latter form of psychic
life is the path of soul transmutation. It is to attain
this state of soul life that the Art of Alchemy is resorted
to. In fact, the transmutation of the soul, contrary to
her *nature,* by energizing her with the action of the mind,
is the Alchemical Transmutation of the soul. Inasmuch
as the mind in man is not distinct from the Mind, but
is in fact an individualized portion of this same Mind,
it follows that any action of the mind in man is an action
of the Mind. As the Mind is the very Essence of God in
the form of radiating energy like the light of the sun,
it will follow that the individualized mind in man is this
same Divine Energy, and that as it acts upon the soul,
the soul is illumined by the Light of God, as the atmos-
phere of the earth is illuminated by the light of the sun.
This means that all thought of the mind is the direct
action of God Himself within our souls, and that as
far as the soul is directed by the mind, she herself
becomes divine in her actions. This will mean that man
is godlike in so far as he is controlled by the thinking
of his own mind. When the soul is absolutely controlled by the mind, becoming perfectly passive to its
action, and no other vibratory force is permitted to
energize her psyche, she is saved and Regenerated, and
there is no other salvation than this. Thus you can see
at a glance, what is meant by the Art of Alchemy when
it is applied to the soul. In these Lessons we are dealing only with the Speculative Art of Alchemy, as we
are not undertaking to tell you how to go about the consummation of the Great Work of Soul Transmutation
at this time, but only to give you an understanding of
the nature of the process. The practical instruction will
be given in the next set of Lessons when we come to deal
with the Practical Art of Alchemy. At the same time,
no one can consummate the Practical Art of Alchemy

until he has mastered the principles of the Speculative Art of Alchemy as we have given them in these Lessons. This Course of Lessons constitutes the Official Text Book of the Hermetic Brotherhood of Atlantis for the study of the Speculative Art of Alchemy, they contain as much of the Sacred Art as will ever be given to the general public at any time. Enough has been said to show the student that in the Hermetic Teaching the purpose was not simply to give theoretical instructions that were to be believed as matters of faith, in the sense of accepting a Creed, a mere matter of a philosophy of life, neither yet was it simply to give a Code of Ethics by which one might regulate his life, but it was something much grander as well as more practical that was aimed at. It was not that they might propitiate certain gods, and thereby gain their favour. The real object of all the teaching and training was to show them how to transmute their souls through the exercise of their mind, and in this way save themselves. Hermes was teaching his sons to save themselves from the dominion of Bad, through self-regeneration and transmutation of the soul. It is also to be borne in mind that he clearly taught the salvation of the soul. He did not teach that souls themselves are good, but he taught how the soul could be purged of bad and could become good through the action of the mind. We have here the most perfect definition of sin and righteousness ever given to man. Sin is the result of the soul permitting herself to be energized by the images of sensibles, while righteousness is the result of her being energized by the images of intelligibles. Salvation is merely the eradication of these images of sensibles from the soul, and their being replaced by the images of intelligibles. The soul is damned through being energized by the sense, and she is saved as a result of her being energized by the thinking of the mind. In this way do we find that the Plan of Salvation advanced by him is perfectly Scientific and Philosophical, and at the same time, there is an Art of Salvation. The Hermetic Psychology is perfect, and is destined ultimately to eliminate all other systems of Psychology. But the crowning glory of this teaching is that Hermes tells us exactly how to do it all ourselves. He places the power of self-regeneration, self-transmutation, and self-salvation within the reach of each and every one of us. The problem of Regeneration is merely a problem of knowing how, and then putting into practice the knowledge that one has attained.

In this training there are three stages of Discipleship. Let it be borne in mind that the Hermetic Discipleship is in realty a course of training. Never make the mistake of assuming that it is merely a theory that you have undertaken to study. If you are serious in your application to the Hermetic Wisdom, you have seriously undertaken the Regeneration and Transmutation of your own soul from humanity to divinity. It is therefore, the Art of self-transmutation that you have undertaken to master. Therefore, it is not enough for you to understand the teaching, you must also actually accomplish the Great Work in yourself. The Three Grades are first, the grade of the Disciple, which is symbolized by Ammon, in this stage of the Disciple, the Master instructs him in the theoretical part of the teaching, while the Disciple preserves an absolute silence, striving to grasp the teachings of the Master; in the second grade, symbolized by Tat, the Disciple becomes a Son of Hermes; in this stage, his instruction is by Dialogue, and he is permitted to ask questions: the Master is the Father of the Son, and is in a sense as God to the Sons, who are energized by his ideas, and made to become like unto him. When they have reached that state of Initiation symbolized by the Mountain Top, and are able to behold the Truth with the Gnostic Eye as it were, they pass through the Virgin Birth, which admits them to the Third

Stage. This is the stage or Grade of the Companions of Hermes, symbolized by Asclepius, where they are treated by the Master as equals, and where they discuss and argue the points of the Teaching. The Disciple is a student of the Theoretical Side of the Hermetic Logos, the Son is a student of the Applied aspect of the Hermetic Logos, but the Companion is under training in the Technical Work, and is what we might term an Apprentice Workman. When he has accomplished this training and has mastered the Technical Art of Self-regeneration, he is admitted to the Sublime Fourth Grade and is a Master Workman, and is no longer in need of training, but can in his turn become a Master of Disciples, this Master Grade is symbolized by Hermes himself. These Lessons are for my Sons rather than for my Disciples, and the next series of Lessons, dealing as they will with the Practical Art of Alchemy, will bring them to the Virgin Birth and prepare them for graduation into the Grade of Companions. These Lessons for my Sons are written in the hope that there are in the world many who have reached the status of Sons of Hermes as a result of their making a study of my other Alchemical Works and as a result of the training they may have received in the Brotherhood, or through other sources of training.

A word may not be out of place here, relative to some of the terms made use of in these Lessons. Mind when written with a capital letter means the Common or General Mind, Mind in the sense of the radiating energy of God, Mind as Principle. When it is written with a small letter as mind, it means this same Mind individualized and energizing a human soul, as a human mind. Reason when written with a capital letter is the Cosmic Logos working in conjunction with the Mind. When it is written with a small letter it is used for the same Logos functioning as the reason in a man, such reason working in conjunction with his mind. Soul when written with a

capital letter is the Universal Soul or Psyche as a
Principle, but if written with a small letter it is the
same Principle individualized as the soul of a man. And
so with Spirit, and Body and Life. Matter may be
used either as being the Primal Substance as the Maternal Principle which gives birth to all things,
or it may be Physical Matter. Thought written with
a capital letter is a Thought of the Mind, while if
written with a small letter it means the thought of a
human mind. Ideas when written with a capital letter
refer to the Thought-forms engendered by the Cosmic
Logos, while if written with a small letter they refer to
the forms produced by the reason in man for the expression of the thoughts of his mind. Intelligibles are those
things which we can perceive by reason of the action
of our intelligence, that is with the mind and reason,
but cannot perceive with the senses. Sensibles are those
things that can be perceived by the action of the senses,
either of the senses of the body, of the spirit, or of the
soul. Spirit is used in a sense nearly the same as Astral
is used by a great many writers on such subjects. The
other terms are sufficiently explained in the body of the
Lessons, so that they will not require any other explanation here.

The writer has tried to make his meaning clear all
the way through the Lessons, and feels sure that all real
students will be able to understand him. Of course, no
one will be able to understand these Lessons, unless they
have mastered the teaching that has been previously
given. Let the student first master Philosophia Hermetica, then Scientifica Hermetica, then the Hermetic
Art, then The Philosophy of Alchemy, then the Science
of Alchemy, and then and then only will he be ready
for these Lessons on the Speculative Art of Alchemy.
If he finds these Lessons incomplete, let him not give up,
but realize that the practical instructions are to be found

in the next set of Lessons, which deal with The Practical Art of Alchemy. Here we must bid farewell to those who have merely been interested in Speculative Occultism, only those having the supreme courage to enter the field of Practical Occultism need go any farther with us. If you want to go on, and make your self the equal of the immortal gods, then continue your studies, but from now on, you must learn to Do, to Will, to Dare and to Keep Silent, your period of Learning is over, henceforth, if you continue you must enter the life of Action and the Quest for Power, only Supermen can be Practical Alchemical Artists

DR. A. S. RALEIGH.

Berros, Calif., February 20th, 1918.

THE SPECULATIVE ART OF ALCHEMY
ABOUT THE COMMON MIND
TEXT

Parthey (G) *Hermetis Trismegisti Poemander* (Berlin, 1854), 99-113;

Patrizzi (F) *Nova de Universis Philosophia* (Venis, 1593) 23b-25b;

Mead (G. R. S.) *Thrice Greatest Hermes* (London, 1906), Corpus Hermeticum XII (XIII).

1. *Hermes.* The Mind, O Tat, is of God's very essence—(if such a thing as *essence* of God there be)—and what *that* is, it and it only knows precisely.

The Mind, then, is not separated off from God's essentiality, but is united unto it, as light to sun.

This Mind in men is God, and for this cause some of mankind are gods, and their humanity is nigh unto divinity.

For the Good Daimon said: "Gods are immortal men, and men are mortal gods."

2. But in irrational lives Mind is their *nature.* For where is Soul, there too is Mind; just as where Life, there is there also Soul.

But in irrational lives their soul is life devoid of mind; for Mind is the in-worker of the souls of men for good;—He works on them for their own good.

In lives irrational He doth co-operate with each one's nature, but in the souls of men He counteracteth them.

For every soul, when it becomes embodied, is instantly depraved by pleasure and by pain.

For in a compound body, just like juices, pain and pleasure seethe, and into them the soul, on entering in, is plunged.

3. O'er whatsoever souls the Mind doth, then, preside, to these it showeth its own light, by acting counter to their prepossessions, just as a good physician doth upon the body prepossessed by sickness, pain inflict, burning or lancing it for sake of health.

In just the selfsame way the Mind inflicteth pain upon the soul, to rescue it from pleasure, whence comes its every ill.

The great ill of the soul is godlessness; then followeth fancy for all evil things and nothing good.

So, then, Mind counteracting it doth work good on the soul, as the physician health upon the body.

4. But whatsoever human souls have not the Mind as pilot, they share in the same fate as souls of lives irrational.

For [Mind] becomes co-worker with them, giving full play to the desires towards which [such souls] are borne—[desires] that from the rush of lust strain after the irrational; [so that such human souls,] just like irrational animals, cease not irrationally to rage and lust, nor ever are they satiate of ills.

For passions and irrational desires are ills exceeding great; and over these God hath set up the Mind to play the part of judge and executioner.

5. *Tat.* In that case, father mine, the teaching (*logos*) as to Fate, which previously thou didst explain to me, risks to be over-set.

For that if it be absolutely fated for a man to fornicate, or commit sacrilege, or do some other evil deed, why is he punished,—when he hath done the deed from Fate's necessity?

Her. All works, my son, are Fate's; and without
Fate naught of things corporal—or good, or ill—can
come to pass.

But it is fated too, that he who doeth ill, shall suffer. And for this cause he doth it—that he may suffer what he suffereth, because he did it.

6. But for the moment, [Tat,] let be the teaching (*logos*) as to vice and Fate, for we have spoken
of these things in other [of our sermons]; but now
our teaching (*logos*) is about the Mind;—what Mind
can do, and how it is [so] different—in men being
such and such, and in irrational lives [so] changed;
and [then] again that in irrational lives it is not of
a beneficial nature, while that in men it quencheth
out the wrathful and the lustful elements.

Of men, again, we must class some as led by reason, and others as unreasoning.

7. But all men are subject to Fate, and genesis
and change, for these are the beginning and the end
of Fate.

And though all men do suffer fated things, those
led by reason (those whom we said the Mind doth
guide) do not endure like suffering with the rest; but,
since they've freed themselves from viciousness, not
being bad, they do not suffer bad.

Tat. How meanest thou again, my father? Is not
the fornicator bad; the murderer bad; and [so with]
all the rest?

Her. [I mean not that;] but that the Mind-led
man, my son, though not a fornicator, will suffer just
as though he had committed fornication, and though
he be no murderer, as though he had committed
murder.

The quality of change he can no more escape than that of genesis.

But it *is* possible for one who hath the Mind, to free himself from vice.

8. Wherefore I've ever heard, my son, Good Daimon also say—(and had He set it down in written words, He would have greatly helped the race of men; for He alone, my son, doth truly, as the First-born God, gazing upon all things, give voice to words (*logoi*) divine)—yea, once I heard Him say:

"All things are one, and most of all the bodies which the mind alone perceives. Our life is owing to [God's] Energy and Power and Æon. His Mind is Good, so is His Soul as well. And this being so, intelligible things know naught of separation. So, then, Mind, being Ruler of all things, and being Soul of God, can do whate'er it wills."

9. So do thou understand, and carry back this word (*logos*) unto the question thou didst ask before, —I mean about Mind's Fate.

For if thou dost with accuracy, son, eliminate [all] captious arguments (*logoi*), thou wilt discover that of very truth the Mind, the Soul of God, doth rule o'er all—o'er Fate, and Law, and all things else; and nothing is impossible to it,—neither o'er Fate to set a human soul, nor under Fate to set [a soul] neglectful of what comes to pass. Let this so far suffice from the Good Daimon's most good [words].

Tat. Yea, [words] divinely spoken, father mine, truly and helpfully. But further still explain me this.

10. Thou said'st that Mind in lives irrational worked in them as [their] nature, co-working with their impulses.

But impulses of lives irrational, as I do think, are passions.

Now if the Mind co-worketh with [these] impulses, and if the impulses of [lives] irrational be passions, then is Mind also passion, taking its colour from the passions.

Her. Well put, my son! Thou questionest right nobly, and it is just that I as well should answer [nobly].

11.   All things incorporal when in a body are subject unto passion, and in the proper sense they are [themselves] all passions.

For every thing that moves [another] is incorporal; while every thing that's moved is body.

Incorporals are further moved by Mind, and movement's passion.

Both, then, are subject unto passion—both mover and the moved, the former being ruler and the latter ruled.

But when a man hath freed himself from body, then is he also freed from passion.

But, more precisely, son, naught is impassible, but all are passible.

Yet passion differeth from passibility; for that the one is active, while the other's passive.

Incorporals moreover act upon themselves, for either they are motionless or they are moved; but whichsoe'er it be, it's passion.

But bodies are invariably acted on, and therefore are they passible.

Do not, then, let terms trouble thee; action and passion are both the selfsame thing. To use the fairer sounding term, however, does no harm.

12.   *Tat.* Most clearly hast thou, father mine, set

forth the teaching (*logos*).

Her. Consider this as well, my son; that these two things God hath bestowed on man beyond all mortal lives—both mind and speech (*logos*) equal to immortality. He hath the mind for knowing God," and uttered speech (*logos*) for eulogy of Him.

And if one useth these for what he ought, he'll differ not a whit from the immortals. Nay, rather, on departing from the body, he will be guided by the twain unto the Choir of Gods and Blessed Ones.

13. *Tat.* Why, father mine!—do not the other lives make use of speech (*logos*)?

Her. Nay, son; but use of voice; speech is far different from voice. For speech is general among all men, while voice doth differ in each class of living thing.

Tat. But with men also, father mine, according *to* each race, speech differs.

Her. Yea, son, but man is one; so also speech is one and is interpreted, and it is found the same in Egypt, and in Persia, and in Greece.

Thou seemest, son, to be in ignorance of Reason's (*Logos*) worth and greatness. For that the Blessed God, Good Daimon, hath declared:

"Soul is in Body, Mind in Soul; but Reason (*Logos*) is in Mind, and Mind in God; and God is Father of [all] these."

14. The Reason, then, is the Mind's image, and Mind God's [image]; while Body is [the image] of the Form; and Form [the image] of the Soul.

The subtlest part of Matter is, then, Air; of Air, Soul; of Soul, Mind; and of Mind, God.

And God surroundeth all and permeateth all; while Mind surroundeth Soul, Soul Air, Air Matter.

Necessity and Providence and Nature are instruments of Cosmos and of Matter's ordering; while of intelligible things each is Essence, and Sameness is their Essence.

But of the Bodies of the Cosmos each is many; for though possessing Sameness, [these] composed Bodies, though they do change from one into another of themselves, do natheless ever keep the incorruption of their Sameness.

15. Whereas in all the rest of composed bodies, of each there is a certain number; for without number structure cannot be, or composition, or decomposition.

Now it is units that give birth to number and increase it, and, being decomposed, are taken back again into themselves.

Matter is one; and this whole Cosmos—the mighty God and image of the mightier One, both with Him unified, and the conserver of the Will and Order of the Father—is filled full of Life.

Naught is there in it throughout the whole of Æon, the Father's [everlasting] Re-establishment, —nor of the whole, nor of its parts,—which doth not live.

For not a single thing that's dead, hath been, or is, or shall be in [this] Cosmos.

For that the Father willed it should have Life as long as it should be. Wherefore it needs must be a God.

16. How, then, O son, could there be in the God, the image of the Father, in the plentitude of Life— dead things?

For that death is corruption, and corruption is destruction.

How then could any part of that which knoweth no corruption be corrupted, or any whit of him the God destroyed?

Tat. Do they not, then, my father, die—the lives in it, that are its parts?

Her. Hush, son!—led into error by the term in use for what takes place.

They do not die, my son, but are dissolved as compound bodies.

Now dissolution is not death, but dissolution of a compound; it is dissolved not so that it may be destroyed, but that it may become renewed.

For what is the activity of life? Is it not motion? What then in Cosmos is there that hath no motion? Naught is there, son!

17. *Tat.* Doth not Earth even, father, seem to thee to have no motion?

Her. Nay, son; but rather that she is the only thing which, though in very rapid motion, is also stable.

For how would it not be a thing to laugh at, that the Nurse of all should have no motion, when she engenders and brings forth all things?

For 'tis impossible that without motion one who doth engender, should do so.

That thou shouldst ask if the fourth part is not inert, is most ridiculous; for that the body which doth have no motion, gives sign of nothing but inertia.

18. Know, therefore, generally, my son, that all that is in Cosmos is being moved for decrease or for increase.

Now that which is kept moving, also lives; but there is no necessity that that which lives, should be all same.

For being simultaneous, the Cosmos, as a whole, is not subject to change, my son, but all its parts are subject unto it; yet naught [of it] is subject to corruption, or destroyed.

It is the terms employed that confuse men. For 'tis not genesis that constituteth life, but 'tis sensation; it is not change that constituteth death, but 'tis forgetfulness.

Since, then, these things are so, they are immortal all,—Matter, [and] Life, [and] Spirit, Mind [and] Soul, of which whatever liveth, is composed.

19.   Whatever then doth live, oweth its immortality unto the Mind, and most of all doth man, he who is both recipient of God, and coessential with Him.

For with this life alone doth God consort; by visions in the night, by tokens in the day, and by all things doth He foretell the future unto him,—by birds, by inward parts, by wind, by tree.

Wherefore doth man lay claim to know things past, present and to come.

20.   Observe this, too, my son; that each one of the other lives inhabiteth one portion of the Cosmos, —aquatic creatures water, terrene earth, and aery creatures air; while man doth use all these,—earth, water, air, [and] fire; he seeth heaven, too, and doth contact it with [his] sense.

But God surroundeth all, and permeateth all, for He is energy and power; and it is nothing difficult, my son, to *conceive* God.

21.   But if thou wouldst Him also *contemplate*, behold the ordering of the Cosmos, and [see] the orderly behaviour of its ordering; behold thou the Necessity of things made manifest, and [see] the Providence of things become and things becoming; behold

how Matter is all-full of Life; [behold] this so great
God in movement, with all the good and noble [ones]
—gods, daimones and men!

Tat. But these are purely energies, O father mine!

Her. If, then, they're purely energies, my son,—
by whom, then, are they energized except by God?

Or art thou ignorant, that just as Heaven, Earth,
Water, Air, are parts of Cosmos, in just the selfsame
way God's parts are Life and Immortality, [and]
Energy, and Spirit, and Necessity, and Providence,
and Nature, Soul, and Mind, and the Duration of all
these that is called Good?

And there is naught of things that have become, or
are becoming, in which God is not.

22. *Tat.* Is He in Matter, father, then?

Her. Matter, my son, is separate from God, in order that thou may'st attribute unto it the quality of
space. But what thing else than mass think'st thou
it is, if it's not energized? Whereas if it be energized, by whom is it made so? For energies, we said,
are parts of God.

By whom are, then, all lives enlivened? By whom
are things immortal made immortal? By whom
changed things made changeable?

And whether thou dost speak of Matter, or of
Body, or of Essence, know that these too are energies
of God; and that materiality is Matter's energy, that
corporality is Bodies' energy, and that essentiality
doth constitute the energy of Essence; and this is
God—the All.

23. And in the All is naught that is not God.
Wherefore nor size, nor space, nor quality, nor form,
nor time, surroundeth God; for He is All, and All
surroundeth all, and permeateth all.

Unto this Reason *(Logos)*, son, thy adoration and thy worship pay. There is one way alone to worship God; [it is] not to be bad.

LESSON I.

1. *Hermes.* The Mind, O Tat, is of God's very essence—(if such a thing as *essence* of God there be) —and what *that* is, it and it only knows precisely.

The Mind, then, is not separated off from God's essentiality, but is united unto it, as light to sun.

This Mind in men is God, and for this cause some of mankind are gods, and their humanity is nigh unto divinity.

For the Good Daimon said: "Gods are immortal men, and men are mortal gods."

Hermes. The Mind, O Tat, is of God's very essence—(if such a thing as *essence* of God there be)— and what *that* is, it and it only knows precisely.

Mind is declared to be the essence of God. We must bear in mind that in this connection he means the God Beyond all Name, the Ultimate Divine Principle. What he means to state is that we are not entitled to draw a distinction between God and Mind, viewing Mind as something created by God, or even as an Emanation from God, but as being the Essence of God. He expresses some doubt as to the propriety of speaking of the *essence* of God. The difficulty is to express the correct relation between God and the Mind. God is the ultimate Esse. His essence would be this same Esse in action. God as Esse is latency. while Mind is this Latent Esse in activity. Mind as the essence of God is therefore the Divine Esse in action. They are to be thought of as being two stages

(23)

in a seqential process, of one and the same Verity, which
is God. He states that the Mind is the *essence* of God,
while God is the Esse of that *essence,* but as to what
that esse*nce* is, that *essence* alone knows precisely. In
other words, we have no means of knowing the exact
nature of the Essence of God. There being nothing with
which we may compare it, we must think of it merely
as being related to God as *essence* to *its* ultimate Esse.
This Essence is conscious of itself, and through its consciousness of itself, it knows itself, as being itself. In
no other way can it be known. This is the Self-Consciousness of Mind as Essence of God. We can have no
other way of knowing it. Therefore, we may only
speak of it, Mind as being the very essence of God.

The Mind, then, is not separated off from God's essentiality, but is united unto it, as light to sun.

We are, therefore, to realize that the Mind is not something separated off from the essentiality of God, as being
something *other,* but rather that it is something united
unto this essentiality of God, as essentially pertaining
unto it. It is rather difficult to convey the thought here.
Mind is not separated off from God's essentiality as being
other than this essentiality, but being united to this essentiality, it is not the same as that essentiality, seeing that
if it were it would be identical with that essentiality, and
hence could not be united, seeing that the relation of subject and object must subsist before uniting can obtain.
Much use is here made of the Platonic Duality of Same
and Other. God is taken as the basis of all reasoning,
and then, all things are classified as being either the same
as God, or other than God. Of course nothing but God
is the same as God, and hence, all else but God is other
than God. Nothing is the same as anything but its own
essence, it is other than all save itself. No matter in
what department you may delve, you will find this Dual
classification of Same and Other applicable. All things

Born are of necessity, Other than that of which they were born, that is God as Ku the Mother or Bearer, while God only is the Same as God. He means then, that Mind is not separated off from God's essentiality as being something Other than that essentiality. But, as it is united to the essentiality of God, it follows that Mind is not the Same as that essentiality. Then, we appear to have in Mind that Third Category, which is neither Same, nor Other. This however is not possible, save in a very narrow metaphysical sense. It is united unto God's essentiality as light is to the sun, that is, in the same way that the sunlight is united to the sun itself. This will enable us to understand the manner of such union. The light is united to the sun, in the sense of being the radiating energy of the sun itself. It is not something distinct from the sun, being in fact the solar energy itself, hence we can not correctly say it is *other* than the sun, and at the same time, it is not identical with the sun, so that we cannot say that it is the *same* as the sun. We can only speak of it as being the radiating energy of the sun. In like manner, Mind is not identical with the essentiality of God, neither is it separate from that essentiality, hence we can neither speak of it as the *same* as the essentiality of God, or as being *other* than that essentiality. Rather must we think of Mind as being united to the essentiality of God, as the radiating, energy of God, in which His Essentiality is *continued as Mind*. Mind is therefore, the continuation of the essentiality of God, under the form of that essentiality radiating as energy. This being the case, we might speak of Mind as being the Mind of the Essentiality of God, or, possibly better, as being the Essential Mind of God, using God as the Subject Noun, and Mind here as the Predicate Verb, never as an Objective Noun. This should enable you to understand the relation of the Mind as Essence to the essentiality of God's Esse. At least this is as far as any one can make it by explanation, Gnosis of the Mind alone can bring the clear realization.

This Mind in men is God, and for this cause some of mankind are gods, and their humanity is nigh unto divinity.

We are assured that this Mind in men is God. By this we are to understand that God resides in men through the medium of the Mind. We all admit that there is a divine element in man. There is in us something that attunes us with God. We feel that there is a link in our being that keeps us in a state of unity with God. This idea has been expressed by the term "the God within us." Man is conscious of his unity with the Divine, though he does not at all times know what it is that unites him with the Divinity. If there be a divine element in us, it behooves us above all things to discover what it is, in order that we may cultivate it to the highest possible degree. We are assured that this Divine Element is the Mind. When we bear in mind that the Mind is the radiating, active essence of God, we can of course see at once that this, and this only can be the divine element in us. Mind being the radiating essence of God, as we have seen above, radiating from God as its center of radiation, radiating as Centrifugal Force, it must radiate *to* something, as well as radiate *from* something. It radiates from God, hence it must radiate to something which is *other* than God. All Centrifugal Force must become Centripetal Force. Just as a force radiates from a Center, so must this radiation from a Center, cause it to move in the direction of a center or centers. This Mind enters into men, and there becomes the Divine within them, being the God Essence that is resident in them, hence, Mind is not the *same* as man, seeing that it does not originate in man, and does not partake of his nature, but is the divine essence entering into him. At the same time, it is not *other* than man, seeing that it resides within him. Just

as Mind is united to the essentiality of God as light is
to the sun, so is it united to the essentiality of man,
as light is to the earth in daytime. Just as light shines
from the sun into the earth, so does Mind radiate from
the essentiality of God into the essentiality of man. It
is this link of Mind which unites man unto God. Some
of mankind are gods, because of the Divine Element of
Mind resident within them. Mind being the essence of
God, it follows that this essence in man, will endow man
with divine attributes. It will so rule man as to make
him godlike. That man is a god, in whom Mind has been
translated into Will and Action, so that being ruled by
Mind, he is ruled by the essence of God, and hence
is ruled by God, not as a Ruler from without, but as the
ruling Will from within himself. It is this which renders
the essentiality of man Divine and not Human, hence
is man a god; for what is a god but a being whose
essentiality is as the essentiality of God? The humanity
of such a man is nigh unto divinity, that is, it partakes
more of the nature of God than it does of the nature of
man. Such a humanity is that which derives its guiding
principle from the essentiality of the man, which is in
turn determined by Mind. There is so little difference
between the humanity of such a man, and divinity, that
we make no mistake in calling his humanity by the name
of divinity. This divine humanity is nothing other than
a humanity that is but the spontaneous manifestation
of Mind functioning as the essentiality of the man. In
proportion therefore, as a man is ruled by Mind is he
divine while in proportion as Mind does not rule him,
he is human. God-men are merely those men who are
ruled in all that they do, by the indwelling Mind. It is
the influence of Mind that brings man near unto divinity
in all things.

For the Good Daimon said: "Gods are immortal
men, and men are mortal gods."

The Good Daimon here represents the Mind. This is, therefore, the positive declaration of the Mind that the gods are immortal men, while men are mortal gods. This can only mean that the only point where the gods are superior to men, is in the immortality of the former. Likewise, it is only in the mortality of men, that they are inferior to the gods. The meaning of this statement is, the Mind is manifested in men and gods alike, so that neither one possesses any advantage over the other so far as the possession of Mind is concerned. In neither case is Mind the essentiality of gods or men, but in either case is Mind united to the essentiality of both gods and men. This renders the gods and men alike and in an equal degree, the recipients of God's essence, or Mind. The distinction then, between gods and men is not in the Mind which is united to their essentiality, neither in the ability of the Mind to rule the humanity of men and the divinity of the gods, seeing that they are equal in this respect, but in the fact that humanity is the essentiality of men, and divinity the essentiality of the Gods. The real superiority of the gods to men however, is in the fact that men, having bodies of a composed form, which are the product of Becoming, they must of necessity be disintegrated, so that men continue their life through a sequential change of bodies, while the gods, not being the products of Becoming, but being born of Time, have bodies of a finer form and composition, which enables them to be continuously transformed by the Law of Periodic Change, and hence they are able to continue in one body until the time for their ascending to the higher state to which they are destined. It is in his corruptible body more than in any thing else that man is inferior to the gods. The nature of the gods is the same as that of men, only the gods are endowed with immortality, and hence do not experience death. However, it should be understood that this is in the main, owing to the fact that the gods do not possess physical bodies. But, there is likewise a distinction between the spirits of men and of the gods, for in the gods the Life Principle is immortal while in the case of men it is mortal. This excellence of man however, is not to be understood as pertaining to every one of the men, but merely as pertaining to the Human Species, and as being within the reach of man when he has become perfected, we are speaking of the Perfect Man, not of those who are not as yet, come to the status of the full grown man. It is not every man who is a mortal god, but only he who has become perfected as man, the essential man, or the Substantial Man in contradistinction to the material or animal man. We will learn a little later on, the difference between the man of our Sermon, and the ordinary man, who is without Mind in the strictest sense of the word.

2. But in irrational lives Mind is their *Nature*. For where is Soul, there too is Mind; just as where Life, there is there also Soul.

But in irrational lives their soul is life devoid of mind; for Mind is the in-worker of the souls of men for good;—He works on them for their own good.

In lives irrational He doth co-operate with each one's nature; but in the souls of men He counteracteth them.

For every soul, when it becomes embodied, is instantly depraved by pleasure and by pain.

For in a compound body, just like juices, pain and pleasure seethe, and into them the soul, on entering in, is plunged.

But in irrational lives Mind is their *nature*. For where is Soul, there too is Mind; just as where Life, there is there also Soul.

At the same time, we must bear in mind that Mind is not limited to man and to the gods, it is the *nature* of irrational lives. By irrational lives, we are to understand the animals or living ones who are devoid of Reason. The animals have souls, but souls, that have not evolved Reason, this being manifested in man, but in nothing below him in the scale of life. While these animals are without Reason, yet they have Mind in the sense of its being their *nature*. There can no more exist Soul without Mind, than there can Life without Soul. By Life here we are to understand Spirit which is the Vehicle of Life. This Spirit can never be where there is not also a Soul. The Spirit is the connecting link between the Soul and the Body, and therefore, in the absence of a Soul, the Spirit or Life will cease to *be,* seeing that it is merely the energizing of the Soul. Soul is equally dependent upon Mind, for Soul is energized by Mind, which is the true cause of all of the Psychic Operations that go to make up the life of the Soul. This matter will be made clearer as we go on with the interpretation.

But in irrational lives their soul is life devoid of mind; for Mind is the in-worker of the souls of men for good;—He works on them for their own good.

Notwithstanding the fact that Mind is the *Nature* of the irrational lives, yet, their soul is life devoid of mind. Here we have a distinction in the character of Mind. Mind in the sense in which we have been speaking of it, is the radiating energy from the essentiality of God, hence the very essence of God, which is radiated forth, and which is united to the essentiality of gods and men, and in a sense to that of the irrational lives, or animals. In this sense, it is the Common, General or Universal Mind, Mind as a Force or Energy, Mind as Essence, just as Light as a Universal Force is to be conceived of. In this sense, of course, Mind is in every thing in existence, seeing that it is the radiating energy that flows from God into all things. It is thus that God, the Energizer, energizes all things made. But, when this Universal Energy, Mind, has entered into the essentiality of the lives, there is a difference in the manner of its action upon them. In the case of the irrational lives, it acts merely as an energy of a universally diffused character, which becomes their *nature*, without having either taken form, or having been individualized in any manner. Therefore, the irrational life or animal is actuated by Mind as its *nature*, that is, as the *Group Nature* of the entire species, but we would never speak of an animal as having a mind, that is, of individually possessing a mind in the individual sense. In these animals, the Mind is an energy of a universal character, which acting on the soul, becomes its *nature*, but, in no case does Mind become a mind in the sense of the ruling principle back of that soul as is the case with man. When the Mind has been united to the essentiality of man, that is of his soul, it is individualized in accordance with the character and individuality of that soul, so as to become an individual mind, united to that soul, just as the soul is to the spirit. It also becomes the Ruler of the soul, being just as individual as is the soul. This leads to the Mind Consciousness, which is the result of the Self-consciousness of the Mind in man. It is in the possession of individualized mind, or an individual mind that man transcends the irrational souls of the animals. Mind is the inworker of the souls of men for good; He works on them for their own good. This means that when the Mind as energy is joined to the soul of a man, He acts upon the soul in such a manner as to work into it, thus entering within the soul. Thus, Mind entering within the soul, becomes individualized as a mind, which resides within the soul, and working upon it, from within, becomes the active principle, while the soul is reduced to the status of the passive substance on which the active mind is able to work. The mind is now the positive pole, while the soul is the negative pole of this union. The soul is in this way impregnated by the energy of the mind, and conceives as a result of such energizing by the mind. This, in-working of the mind upon the soul, is for good, seeing that good is the essence of the mind but not of the soul, therefore, whatsoever the mind does will be good, seeing that it will be of the essence of the mind to consummate the good, and good can only be established by the action of the mind. The mind is good, but the soul is bad, hence, the soul becomes good in proportion as it is controlled by the energizing of the mind. The mind works on the soul for its own good, that is to say, it is for the good of the soul to be worked upon by the mind, that is, to be energized by the mind, and made to reproduce the mental operations as psychic operations. It is for the good of the soul that this may result, seeing that it makes the soul become good, by making it over into the image and likeness of the mind, and there is nothing so good for the soul as, that she may herself become good. She can only become good by becoming like the mind for that is the only part that is good. The mind works on the soul for good, because this mind of the man is merely the individualized form of the Mind which is radiated from the essentiality of God. It is only in this way that God influences the souls of men, through the action of Mind upon them, and this influence is through their own minds, which are merely so many individual particles of the One Mind. It is through each one's mind then that God doth rule him, and God has no other way of ruling a man save through the mind. From this it will follow that in exact proportion as the soul is controlled by the mind of a man, is he responsive to the influence of God, and in no other way. The distinction between the influence of the Mind upon man and upon the irrational lives is to be seen in this, that, while in the case of the irrational lives or animals, Mind acts upon the surfaces of their souls, influencing them from without, in the case of man, it enters within his soul, becoming an individualized mind, and working upon the soul from within.

In lives irrational He doth co-operate with each one's nature; but in the souls of men He counteracteth them.

In the case of the animals, Mind works in conjunction with their natures, is in fact their nature. To understand this correctly, we must get a key to the meaning of this expression *nature*. What are we to understand the *nature* of anyone to be? The word nature comes from *Natura*, a word which means "the bearing" or the "process of being born." Matter is derived from Materia, that of which things are made, and likewise from Mater-Mother. In other words, Matter is the Mother Substance, which in itself, and of itself, causes itself to assume diverse forms. Mater is the informing Principle which caused Materia to assume the diverse forms which are the basis of *things*. In this sense is Matter the Conceiver, the Gestator, the Bearer and the Primal Substance of all things. Natura is the process of being formed, or of being born, the process of coming into being through the Gestative and Bearing potency of Matter as Mater. It is not the things born, but rather the process of coming into birth. This is the true meaning of *Nature*. The *nature* of any thing is, therefore, the potency of that thing for production, the spontaneity of it for production, what we might term its spontaneous fruitfulness. The inherent power of spontaneous production and reproduction in accordance with an inherent *Norm*, working independent of any outside influence, will therefore, be the *nature* of any thing. From this, we can see at a glance, exactly what constitutes the *nature* of a soul. It is the inherent power of the psyche or soul-substance, to spontaneously produce and bring into being, the types which are inherently present within it. To cause its latency to become activity, and manifest in this way, to produce in accordance with the *Norm* which is inherent in the psyche, without any influencing from any thing else. Its power of self-perpetuation, through eternal renewal. It is the reproduction of the essentiality of the psyche as actual manifestation. This, mind you, is a spontaneous power of the Psyche itself. It is its power of self-evolution from within, through the perpetual unfolding in action of that which is within it, as its essential principle. This principle of spontaneous reproduction is the *modus operandi* of the Law of Karma. This is the *nature* of the soul. Needless to say, this nature can never bring into being, that which is not latently present in the soul herself. It is just as though the soul possesed the power of self-fecundation, and brought forth that which she had conceived within herself. She could in that case not bring forth anything which she of herself could not conceive through the fecundation of herself.

In the case of the animals or irrational lives, the Mind is their *nature,* that is to say, Mind by energizing the souls of these animals, gives to such souls a definite nature, or *involves* that *nature* in their souls, and hence, all subsequent evolution of that animal soul must be along the line of evolving *that* nature. In the case of the animal souls, the Mind doth co-operate with each one's nature, in the sense that the Mind operates through that nature, in all the evolution of the animal. This means that the soul of the animal is not of an individual nature, but of a typal nature, that is to say, the *natures* of all the souls of a given species are of one type, we might say of one nature. It is through this common nature of the type, that the Mind operates. In the case of men, just the reverse is true. The Mind having worked into the soul of man, and there having become individualized as an individual mind, it perpetually impregnates the soul with the germs of action as it were, energizing it, contrary with its nature, but in accord with the essence

of the mind, so as to perpetually *involve*, mental characteristics into the soul. In this way, Mind through the
action of the individual mind, working within the soul,
counteracts the *nature* of the soul, and causes her to act
contrary to her *nature* but in accordence with the energy
of the mind. It is thus, that the mind in man is ever
striving to make the soul obey, and in that way transform the psychic life of that soul into a manifestation
of the mental life of the mind, contrary to the *nature* of
the soul. All *spontaneous* psychic life is the result of
the *nature* of the soul, just as all psychic life which is
the deliberate result of conscious thought, directed unto
that end, is the result of the mind directing the soul,
and energizing her from within. It is for this reason
that in the Religion of the Mind, we are instructed to
suppress all first impulses, all instinctivity, all natural
inclinations, and to at all times, absolutely rule the soul
and all of our psychic life by deliberate and conscious
thought. Mind in the animal works with the nature of
the soul, but in man, It is in perpetual war with the
nature of our souls, striving to make them conform to
the rule of thought. Thus, the animal is ruled by its
nature, but man is ruled by the power of thought.

For every soul, when it becomes embodied, is instantly depraved by pleasure and by pain.

It makes no difference whether the soul be that of a
man or of an animal, the moment it becomes embodied,
or incarnates in a body, it is instantly depraved by pleasure and by pain alike. This leads to the conclusion that
neither pleasure nor pain are sensations properly pertaining to the nature of the soul. So long as the soul
remains in its own sphere, as a soul, free from a body.
it experiences neither pleasure nor pain. Pleasure and
pain are not psychic conditions, properly belonging to
the life of the soul. They are conditions pertaining alone
to the physical plane, and hence to bodies. This being

the case, a soul can only experience pleasure or pain while joined to a body. The moment, however, that the soul enters a body, she is exposed to pleasure and pain. She is now able to feel them both, and thus to receive this experience. The next point for us to bear in mind is this, any experience of pleasure and pain will deprave the soul, from her true nature to the state of the pleasures and pains which she experiences in the body. Thus, while living in the body, the soul can neither follow her own nature, or the influence of the mind, but will be regulated by the pleasures and the pains which she endures. As certain expressions of her nature cause her pain, and others give her pleasure, she will at once, seek to avoid those psychic expressions that cause her pain, and likewise will she seek to repeat those expressions and actions that give pleasure. In this way, will the course of her psychic life be determined by the tendency of her actions to give pleasure or cause pain. In this way will her psychic functioning be warped from its true nature, so as to conform to whatever course will yield the greatest measure of pleasure, and to avoid whatever will cause her pain. As a result, those aspects of her nature that would cause pain if brought into action, are not permitted to express themselves, and as a result, through disuse are dwarfed, while those aspects of her nature, the exercise of which give pleasure, are over-cultivated, and thus become over-developed. It is in this way that life in the body, has the effect of not only turning the soul away from the influence of the mind, but likewise of warping her own nature. This evil is the result of her preferring pleasure to pain. Were she entirely indifferent to pleasure and pain, this effect would not result, but this she cannot be entirely. Asceticism, or that course of discipline where pain is sought in preference to pleasure, is practiced in order that the soul may be brought to subject herself to pain, and by choosing pain in preference to pleasure, she may exercise that part of her nature that brings pain with it. The practice is good, if it is not carried to the extreme. If it is pursued so as to cause her to express the pain giving aspects of her nature, to the same extent as the pleasure bringing aspects, it will be advisable. However, there is the danger of one growing into the state where one finds pleasure in pain, more than in anything else, and then, the soul will become as much warped in the direction of pain, as she formally was in the direction of pleasure. Asceticism should be followed, therefore, as a medicine for the soul, not as a steady diet for her.

For in a compound body, just like juices, pain and pleasure seethe, and into them the soul, on entering in, is plunged.

By a compound body, we are to understand a body made up of diverse elements. It is this composition of the body from the diverse elements, each having its own character, and its own rate of vibration, that causes this warring of the diverse chemical and magnetic forces, response to which, will produce pleasure, and resistence to which will cause pain. These warring forces are termed pleasure and pain, because their action will cause the experience of pleasure and of pain. They seethe in the body, like juices, that is to say, they are there as so many natural juices of the body. This means that we can never eliminate them from the body, seeing that it could not be without them. The very composition of the body depends upon the seething of these forces of pleasure and of pain. As the body can only be held together by them, its composition depending upon them, it will follow that the soul can never enter a body, and there be free from pleasure and pain. When at the time of an incarnation, the soul enters the body, she is at once plunged into these seething forces of pleasure and pain, being as it were Baptised in the seething juices of pleasure and of pain, from that time forth, she is never quite free from pain and likewise is never quite free from pleasure, so long as she remains in the body. It is in this way that the nature of the soul becomes depraved; for this warping influence of pleasure and pain, not only transforms the actions of the soul, but it also transforms her nature, her *natura,* so that the psychic activity stimulated by pleasure and pain, enters into the composition of her *nature* causing it to bring forth in accordance with this transformed state, and not in accordance with the nature given by Mind in the beginning. Of course this causes the greatest possible conflict with the working of the mind, in its efforts to correct the workings of her nature. It is for this reason, that all the time the mind must counteract the nature of the soul in order that man may live the higher life. In the case of the animals, there is no necessity for this counteracting of the nature of the soul, seeing that it is through the influence of pleasure and pain that they evolve, but in the case of the human soul this is not the case.

LESSON II.

3. O'er whatsoever souls the Mind doth, then,
preside, to these it showeth its own light, by acting
counter to their prepossessions, just as a good physician doth upon the body prepossessed by sickness,
pain inflict, burning or lancing it for sake of health.

In just the selfsame way the Mind inflicteth pain
upon the soul, to rescue it from pleasure, whence
comes its every ill.

The great ill of the soul is godlessness; then followeth fancy for all evil things and nothing good.

So, then, Mind counteracting it doth work good on
the soul, as the physician health upon the body.

O'er whatsoever souls the Mind doth, then, preside,
to these it showeth its own light, by acting counter to
their prepossessions, just as a good physician doth
upon the body prepossessed by sickness, pain inflict,
burning or lancing it for sake of health.

The Mind is here spoken of as presiding over certain
souls. We are to understand that the Mind in this connection relates to the Common, General or Universal
Mind which is spoken of as being the very essence of
God. The individualized mind in man is never thought
of as being a separate mind, separated off from the Common Mind, but rather as being the part of that Common
Mind that is functioning in man, being united to his soul.
Thus, man has a soul, but strictly speaking, he has not
a mind, but rather is Mind individualized in him as individual mind, but still as being identical with the Common

(39)

Mind itself. Thus, Mind presides over the soul, through the individual mind that is united to the soul. Any influence which the mind is able to exercise over the soul is therefore spoken of as the Common Mind presiding over that soul. The Mind presides over whatsoever soul, therefore, that is ruled by the individual mind. *All* mental control over a soul is the presiding over that soul, of the Common Mind, which is the Mental Essence of God. The souls over which the Mind presides are merely those souls that are ruled by mind instead of pursuing their own natural trend. To these souls Mind shows its own light, that is to say, these souls are made conscious of that consciousness that is the possession of the Mind. They are illumined by the consciousness of the Mind, and hence have the mental light to guide them and are therefore not limited to the psychic light which comes from the natural function of the psyche herself. This light of the Mind is shown to the soul, when the Mind acts counter to the prepossessions of the soul. Prepossessions are here used in the sense of that which previously possessed the soul before Mind acted upon it. The term is used in the same sense as the prepossession of the body by sickness before the physician undertakes to cure the sickness and establish health in its place. The prepossessions of the soul are therefore the *nature* of the soul, and the natural character of its psychic functioning before Mind acts upon it, in such a manner as to change the course of its action. The Mind acts upon the soul counter to its *natural* trend, and thus, transforms the character of the psychic functioning so as to make it conform to the character of the Mind. It is in this way that the light of Mind is shown to the soul. This action of Mind upon the soul is in every sense of the word a Therapeutic action, as it is calculated to transform the state of the soul, from its natural prepossessions to the Mental condition of light. This process being a curative one, is of necessity, a painful process, just as is the surgical process of curing the ills of the body a painful process. This is of necessity so, because the Mind can only correct and heal the condition of the soul by causing it to yield to the force of Mind, and thereby, completely change the nature of its psychic life from the *natural* to the Mental character.

In just the selfsame way the Mind inflicteth pain upon the soul, to rescue it from pleasure, whence comes its every ill.

All of the ills of the soul are the result of pleasure. This is due to the fact that the nature of the soul and the nature of the body are so diverse that whatever gives pleasure to the body must of necessity be detrimental to the soul, by causing it to become more after the nature of the body. In other words, *while in the body,* the soul derives pleasure only from those vibrations favourable to the expressions of the body's nature. As all others cause it pain, we soon find the soul, yielding to the pleasures of the body, and thus taking pleasure in whatever may give pleasure to the body. Now, all this is of course contrary to the soul's nature, and hence, it causes her to conform herself to the nature of the body, and not to her own nature as a soul. All the ills of the soul are the result of her forsaking her own nature, and conforming to the physical nature, and as this is the result of her seeking pleasure, and doing those things that will give her pleasure, it is, therefore, true that every ill of the soul comes from pleasure. She must be rescued from these pleasures as the only way to save her from these ills. This, therefore, is the problem how to rescue the soul from pleasure in order that she may escape her every ill? When Mind presides over a soul, He inflicteth pain upon her, and in this way, chastising her with pain, draws her away from pleasure, so that through Mind she is disciplined. The means by which this is done is through making all her pleasures painful. This is done

by reason of the vibratory force which the Mind sends
through the soul. All action of the Mind upon the soul
sending through her, a vibratory force which is the exact
opposite of the forces of pleasure, hence, every time
the soul responds to vibratory forces that will give her
pleasure, they run counter to the forces set in motion
by the Mind, and this opposition causes pain. Through
the greater dynamic force of the Mind induced vibratory
forces, the other forces and actions, which give pleasure
to the soul, are counteracted, and are reduced to inac-
tivity. It is in this way that the Mind tends to suppress
all pleasure giving action within the soul. This process
is of course a very painful one, turning all of the pleasures of the soul to pains. It will be painful just so long
as the soul is energized by pleasures of any kind, and
even so long as she follows her own nature. It is the
resistance which the soul offers to the action of the Mind
upon her that renders that action so painful. She can
escape this pain only by perfectly responding to this
action of the Mind; but this she cannot do so long as she
is energized by the forces of pleasure. Of course it will
follow that the pain inflicted by the vibratory forces set
in motion by the action of the Mind will be in exact
proportion to the degree of resistance which they meet
within the soul, owing to the strength of the pleasure
giving forces that are energizing the soul. It is the
action of the Mind upon the soul that causes this pain,
and the pain will increase in proportion to the degree of
such action of the Mind upon the soul, and likewise with
the degree of inharmony of the soul with the Mind.
Bear this in mind, it is utterly out of the question for
the Mind to act upon the soul to any extent whatsoever,
without inflicting pain upon the soul. The soul becomes
the battle ground between the body and the Mind, but
owing to the higher vibratory forces of the Mind, it will
afflict the soul with such severe pains that she will have
to yield to the Mental forces. In this way is she chastised

and whipped by the Mind until she obeys and is governed
by the Mind. In this way, is the soul rescued from
pleasure through the infliction of pain upon her whenever she gives way to, or in any way experiences pleasure.
Thus, she in time, reaches the point where she has no
longer any pleasure, and thus she no longer has any ill.
These pains it should be borne in mind are not physical
pains experienced by the body, but what is far more
painful, psychic pains inflicted upon and within the soul
herself. It is only when the psychic pain of the soul
becomes so great as to overflow her and react upon the
body, that the latter experiences physical pain in connection with the psychic pains of the soul.

The great ill of the soul is godlessness; then followeth fancy for all evil things and nothing good.

Godliness means godlikeness, or the quality of being
like God, as well as the quality of being filled with the
energy of God. Godlessness is just the reverse; it means
not having God, being without God, and hence, the
absence of the energy of God from the godless thing.
The godlessness of the soul, relates to a condition of the
soul, where the energy of God is absent from the soul,
she being empty of the divine energy and in that sense
being empty of God. A godless soul then, will be one
that is not to any extent energized by the energy of
God. A soul, the energy of which is not of God, but of
some lower order. Now, we have seen how it is that the
Mind is both the Essence of God, and likewise the radiating energy of God, and hence, it will follow that a soul
empty of the energy of God, will be one empty of Mind,
hence, godlessness is equivalent to mindlessness. Godlessness is, therefore, characteristic of all souls following
their own *nature,* or governed by pleasures, and not
dominated by the action of Mind, through which they
may be energized by God. This godlessness of the soul
is her greatest ill, and the one requiring eradication

more than any other. This is the status of any soul not
dominated in all of her actions by Mind. After this
greatest ill of godlessness, the next great ill of the soul
is fancy for all evil things and nothing good. Evil is
that which separates from good, and hence, it will have
reference to whatever will absorb one to the extent of
drawing one away from the good, which is that which
is of God. The soul, through fancy, images within herself, the evil things of the world, so that they are made,
through her fancy to abide within herself, as being a
part of herself. Through the senses of the body, and
likewise the senses of the soul, she is able to perceive
objects, these objects of sense, whether physical or
psychic, she through fancy, reproduces within herself,
that is, she forms within herself the *Ideas*, or psychic
images of them. Thus she forms within herself, an ideal
world which exactly corresponds to the objective world
of the senses. This exercise of her fancy, fills her with
the images of all evil things, in the sense of all things
contrary to God, with the images of the senses, but does
not image within her, the images of the divine reality,
hence she has this fancy for all evil things but not for
any good. Through her fancy the soul is made merely
a receptacle for the imaging of the objects of sense, and
being energized by those images, she is made to conform
to them in all her psychic life, seeing that her psychic
life becomes nothing other than so many psychical reactions to the stimulation of these images. Thus her direct
action is replaced by the reaction of the psyche to the
energy of these psychic images.

So, then, Mind counteracting it doth work good on
the soul, as the physician health upon the body.

Mind, when presiding over the soul, counteracts all
of this evil condition. The godlessness of the soul is
counteracted by the Mind, because the Mind is both the
very essence of God and likewise the radiating energy

from His essentiality, hence, the action of Mind upon the soul, has the effect of energizing her with the energy of God. This fills her with that energy of God, so that the absence of that, or her state of godlessness is counteracted, and she being filled with the energy of God and energized thereby, becomes godly and not godless. Her state of godlessness is counteracted and replaced by a state of godliness. The soul being energized by the energy of God or by Mind, has her nature transformed so that she acts in harmony with the essence of God. Likewise, the Mind acting upon the soul, counteracts her fancy, transforming it, from objects of sense, and hence from evil things to the good things, causing it to image the thoughts of the Mind. In this way, are the Ideas of the Cosmos made the Ideas or psychic Images of the soul. She being taught of the Mind, has given to her an ideal world that is the correspondence of the Ideal World of the Cosmos. In this way is she redeemed from the lower world and from the senses of the body as well as from her own senses. In this way does the action of the Mind work good on the soul, by making her good, through her transformation in harmony with the workings of the Mind. This is what it means to have a good soul, as well as for the soul to be converted and to be saved, she must be transformed by the action of the Mind, and her fancy must be so controlled by the Mind, as to build within her, a duplicate of the Ideal World of the Logos. This will of course mean that the soul is born again of the Mind, the Mind being in a sense the Mother of the soul. This is the true meaning of the Discipline of the soul by the Mind. Needless to say this process of transforming the soul will be a very painful one. It is through the infliction of fearful pains upon the soul that the Mind is able to heal her, and to bring her into the state of godliness and piety, which is the result of her being passive under the influence and action of the Mind.

4. But whatsoever human souls have not the Mind
as pilot, they share in the same fate as souls of lives
irrational.

For [Mind] becomes co-worker with them, giving
full play to the desires towards which [such souls]
are borne,—[desires] that from the rush of lust strain
after the irrational; [so that such human souls,]
just like irrational animals, cease not irrationally to
rage and lust, nor ever are they satiate of ills.

For passions and irrational desires are ills exceeding great; and over these God hath set up the Mind to
play the part of judge and executioner.

But whatsoever human souls have not the Mind as
pilot, they share in the same fate as souls of lives irrational.

In the previous section, we have been examining the
condition of the souls over which the Mind presides, and
which are disciplined by it. In this section we are to
see the true status of such human souls as are not ruled
by the Mind. These are spoken of as those human souls
that have not the mind as pilot. This means that they
are not directed by the Mind, but, on the other hand,
expresses their psychic life independent of the Mind's
guidance. What is stated in this section in reference
to the status of such souls will, therefore, apply to all
souls that are not under the guidance of the Mind, and
hence are able to lead their own psychic life without
any of the counteracting force of the Mind, all souls
undisciplined by the Mind in fact. We have seen what
it means for a soul to be disciplined by the Mind, and
the character of such discipline, as well as the effect
upon the soul, when she is healed by the pain inflicted
upon her by the Mind; what is said here as to the condition of other souls will apply to all souls that cannot
be classed according to the specifications given in the

preceding section. Not having the Mind as pilot, they are deprived of Her direction, and thus have to depend upon their own light alone for guidance, and must, therefore, direct their own course as best they can, unaided by the superior light of Mind. We are assured that such souls share in the same fate as lives irrational, that is, the fate of such souls is identical with that of the irrational animals. They derive no advantage from the fact that they are human souls. This statement means nothing more or less than to state that any human soul that is not piloted by the Mind, is in fact no better off than the soul of an irrational animal. Although such souls are human, they lead the same psychic life as do the souls of animals. It is of the greatest importance that we understand how it is that the soul, of itself, unguided by Mind, is unable to live above the psychology of an animal. One point which we simply must grasp is this, the superiority of the human soul to the soul of an animal then, rests not, in any innate superiority of the psyche of which the human soul is composed to the psyche of which the animal soul is composed, seeing that in either case, the psyche is of the same value, but solely in the fact that the animal soul is not guided and piloted by Mind, but acts only of its own force, while the human soul is guided and piloted by Mind. This being true, it will follow that a human soul under the action of its own nature, having not the Mind as pilot will in no case experience a fate superior to that of an animal, seeing that the psychology of such a human soul will be purely that of an animal soul.

For [Mind] becomes co-worker with them, giving full play to the desires towards which [such souls] are borne,—[desires] that from the rush of lust strain after the irrational; [so that such human souls], just like irrational animals, cease not irrationally to rage and lust, nor ever are they satiate of ills.

This paragraph deals with that type of human soul in which the Mind has not been fully individualized so as to become an individual mind, hence, in their case it has to act as the Common Mind does in the case of animals, though to a somewhat less extent than it does in the case of the animals. In the case of these souls, Mind does not rule the soul, but is made use of by the soul, the soul being the positive element that controls the Mind in a sense. These are souls in which the forces of pleasure are so great as to drive the energies of the Mind with them, thus, the Mind is made to become the co-worker with the soul, actually aiding the soul in the reaching of her end, rather than guiding and directing her. The Mind in this way is made to work with the soul in very much the same way that it does in the case of the irrational animals. Mind here becomes incorporated in the nature of the soul, being used by that nature, as though it was the intelligent part of the soul nature rather than the pilot presiding over all the actions of the soul. This being the case, we are dealing here with any soul that possesses Mind merely as an aspect of the soul, and where Mind does not preside over the soul as a higher principle being at one with the Common Mind of the all, the essence of God. We are here speaking of those souls in which Mind is drawn down into the soul, becoming in a sense, a part of that soul, instead of being the pilot over it, to direct its psychic action. In the case of such a soul, Mind is merely manifesting as the intelligent part of the soul, and as such, it is very similar to a faculty of the soul. Hence, it will co-operate with the soul in all things, its course of action being determined by the nature of the soul. In the case of such souls, Mind co-works with them, so as to give full play to the desires towards which the souls are borne.

This is due to the fact that owing to the greater intensity
of the vibration engendered by the action of Mind on
psyche, the soul is made to vibrate much more rapidly
than it would do, were it not for the action of
Mind upon it, which results in a much greater intensity of action on the part of the soul than would be
possible were it not for the action of Mind. The souls
of which we are speaking, being entirely dominated by
the desires for that which gives pleasure, that is, for
those vibrations and energies set in motion by the senses,
and which thereby arouse pleasurable sensations in the
soul, are borne along by such desires. This causes the
souls to yield themselves completely to the energizing
of those pleasures, so as to become manifestations of
those sensations. Mind hastens the process of the soul
in its descent along the path of such desires. These
desires of the soul, cause her to lust after that which
gives her pleasure, that is, after the sensations aroused
in her by the senses of the body, as well as by her own
senses. This lusting of the desires causes the soul to
perpetually image those objects of sense that we have
previously spoken of, and to dwell upon them at all
times, meditating upon them in her interior states, so
that these images created by fancy, are made to live
within her. Mind is drawn into them, so that they are
rendered intelligent, and thus the soul becomes in her
interior, a perfect menagerie of such animals created
within her through the exercise of her fancy in connection with her senses. All her desires are taken up with
these images of things, so that her forces rush after
them with a great lust for them. This causes her desires
to strain after the irrational. These things are called
irrational, because they are contrary to Reason, pertaining to the realm of the senses. Thus, the soul unguided
by Reason, fails to discriminate between the Real and
the Apparent, and strains and lusts after those images
of things of a sensible nature, the Mind being drawn

into those sensible images, so that there is no part of the soul straining after intelligible ideas. In this way, is the soul entirely taken up with the images and ideas of things irrational, being entirely absorbed in the sensation of them, she is in no wise occupied with the Ideas of an Intelligible character, and hence, she is withdrawn from the rational field of life. Such souls become just like irrational animals. They never cease to irrationally rage and lust, that is, to rage and lust after the images of sensibles, and after the objects of their senses as well as of the senses of their bodies. They rage and lust in their efforts to secure that which is contrary to Reason, bringing themselves into a state of complete dependence with that body of sensations which is contrary to Reason, so as to become completely absorbed in it. In this way, their psychic life becomes nothing more than the psychical reactions to the stimulus of the senses. In this way, their psychology becomes that of an animal precisely, but with all the added force and power of a human soul plus the great force of Mind. They therefore become in reality, nothing but super-animal souls, in their animality exceeding the animal soul as much as does the Mind-piloted human soul exceed the animal soul in his greatness. Such souls are never satiate of ills, but as they yield to all the ills, those ills being imaged within them, grow and demand greater and ever greater yielding of the soul to the force of all the ills. As a result, there is no turning back, but a perpetual advance along the path of complete surrender to the desires that lead the soul, enamoured of pleasure, down into the pit of dependence upon the sensations and desires, hence she is depressed more and more into the state of animality, instead of rising up to the status of the Mind she sinks down into the condition of the body.

For passions and irrational desires are ills exceeding great; and over these God hath set up the Mind to play the part of judge and executioner.

By passions, we are to understand those violent out-rushings of the soul and spirit, rushing after things, they are the positive counterparts of the negative desires. By irrational desires, we should understand the negative, centripetal forces of the soul and spirit, which attract, and draw in, that which is contrary to Reason. Passions and irrational desires, as applied to the soul, therefore, refer to the centrifugal motions of the soul in the direction of the objects of sense, driving the psyche after them, and to the centripetal motions of the soul, which draw into her, the energies of the objects of sense causing the imaging of those sensibles in the soul, and the energizing of those sensible images, by the energies of the sensible objects. As all sensibles are contrary to the true Reason, these desires are for that which is irrational, or contrary to Reason, hence they are called irrational desires. Such passions and irrational desires are ills exceeding great, for the reason that they bind the soul completely to the objects of sense, and fill her with the images of sensibles, so that she is completely energized by the energies of sensibles, and in this way is drawn away from the guidance of Reason, so as to become completely irrational in all of her psychic life. They are ills exceeding great for the reason that, if persisted in, they will render the soul completely irra-tional, and completely sensible, binding her to sensibles, and cutting her off entirely from intelligibles, which is an exceeding great ill for the soul; for what can be a greater ill for the soul than that she should be bound to sensations, and have all her psychic life entirely depend-ent upon sensations, contrary to her nature? It is over these passions and irrational desires that God has set up the Mind to play the part of judge and executioner. Mind, by giving its full power to the play of these pas-sions and irrational desires, so intensifies their action that the soul rushes into them with a force so great, as to make of her, a mirror for the reflection of all the sensibles of the universe, so as to become a mere medium for the expression of all the sensations possible. She senses them all and feels them with a sensibility far greater than is possible for anything else to feel them, and this of course arouses the greatest possible amount of pain within her. In the course of time, this process becomes so painful, as to become destructive, unto the end that, these very passions and irrational desires become the means of their own destruction. The disintegrating force becomes so violent that in the course of time, the soul is rendered so fluidic as to be responsive to the transforming influences of the Mind. Thus Mind by co-working with the passions and irrational desires of the soul, is able to destroy them completely, and in that way does she execute them. Mind is the judge of the passions and irrational desires and through her cooperation with them, she hastens their destruction, so that the soul is through her exceeding great pain, driven from them, unto the end that all her desires may become rational, and thus she may become the mirror of the true Reason, and her passions may turn to love, making of her the receptacle of the Ideas of the Reason, imaged in her.

LESSON III.

MIND AND FATE.

5. *Tat.* In that case, father mine, the teaching (*logos*) as to Fate, which previously thou didst explain to me, risks to be over-set.

For that if it be absolutely fated for a man to fornicate, or commit sacrilege, or do some other evil deed, why is he punished,—when he hath done the deed from Fate's necessity?

Her. All works, my son, are Fate's; and without Fate naught of things corporal—or good, or ill—can come to pass.

But it is fated too, that he who doeth ill, shall suffer. And for this cause he doth it—that he may suffer what he suffereth, because he did it.

Tat. In that case, father mine, the teaching (*logos*) as to Fate, which previously thou didst explain to me, risks to be over-set.

Tat here expresses the opinion that if the teaching in regard to the function of the Mind as judge and executioner over the passions and the irrational desires of the soul be true, this would over-set the teaching in regard to Fate. He cannot see how it is possible for one to think that all things are the work of Fate and at the same time to think that there can be any such thing as judgment over the actions which themselves spring from Fate. His difficulty is the same as that of the vast majority of people to-day, who cannot understand the Religion of the Mind, because they cannot see how Fate and Moral Agency can be reconciled, and they assume that judgment and execution of punishment in any form involves the idea of Moral Agency. This was Tat's difficulty, and if we can dispose of this difficulty in the mind of Tat, we will have removed the principle obstacle in the way of an acceptation of the Religion of the Mind.

For that if it be absolutely fated for a man to fornicate, or commit sacrilege, or do some other evil deed, why is he punished,—when he hath done the deed from Fate's necessity?

Here Tat voices the view of Fate that is held by many at the present time. Many Christians believe that it is predestined that a man shall be guilty of certain definite sins, and that there is absolutely nothing that he can do to avoid their commission. If it is predestined from the foundation of the earth that he must commit those identical sins, then, the question is asked, how can he be adjudged guilty of sins which he was required to commit? Again, there are Hindus who think that the Karma of a man will compel him to do certain definite things, and hence, how can he be adjudged guilty of these sins one may ask? Tat asks the question: if it be absolutely fated that a man is to be guilty of a particular sin, then he has no choice in the matter, but must do this of Fate's necessity, being driven into this deed by a power which he is unable to resist, it is evident that he has exercised no power of choice in the matter, and hence, not having chosen this course of his own will and choice; how can he be punished for something which was not of his own selection? He assumes that without Moral Agency, one cannot be justly punished for his acts. His line of reasoning is something like this: if man is a moral agent, he has the power to select between good and evil deeds, and hence, what good deeds he performs are acts of his own choice through which he has deliberately choosen

good in preference to evil, and hence he is entitled to a
reward for his virtue in preferring the good to the evil,
likewise, when he is guilty of an evil deed, it is an act of
his own choice, through which he has deliberately chosen
evil in preference to good, and hence, he should be punished for his wickedness in preferring evil to good.
Punishment is therefore, regarded as the just retribu-
tion for an act of the free will, through which it prefers
evil to good, also, it is thought a corrective in some
instances to cause one to choose the good, in order to
escape the punishment that a choice of the evil would
bring upon him. In this way, the arousing of fear in
the sinner is one of the grounds for advocating punishment. But, if there is no such thing as moral agency,
if one's conduct is determined by Fate, over which he
has no control, if he has no power of choice, and does
evil not because he prefers it to good, but because of
necessity, which he has no power to resist, the question
is: how can he be guilty, and why should he be punished
for something which is no fault of his? This is the
problem which Tat presents, and we are bound to admit
that the solution of that problem is of as great interest
to us today, as it was in his time. The real question is
this: is punishment related to moral agency, or is it with
reference to something else?

Her. All works, my son, are Fate's; and without
Fate naught of things corporal—or good, or ill—can
come to pass.

Hermes does not flinch from the problem, but frankly
states that all works are the works of Fate, there being
nothing ever come into being that Fate has not brought
into being. There is no power other than Fate to cause
anything to be, or to prevent anything from coming into
being if its being is ordained by Fate. This being true,
there is no exercise of the human will that can possibly
bring into being a condition that has not been necessitated

by Fate, or that can prevent the consummation of a condition that has been necessitated by Fate. He goes on to show that this work of Fate applied with equal force to all things corporal, that is to all things relating to bodies, and hence to physical existence, to all good things, that is, things in harmony with the welfare of the soul; and to all ill, or all things detrimental to the welfare of the soul. He does not try to defend moral agency, he deliberately sweeps it out of existence, and leaves man helpless in the hands of Fate. All his deeds are the result of the necessity of Fate, and hence, there can be no such thing as moral responsibility for any of our deeds. There is no qualified necessity of Fate here; but the absolute dominion of Fate, and there is no way by which one may escape it. If punishment is just, we must therefore find some other basis for it than moral agency, seeing that the soul has no power of choice between the two—good and evil. There being no moral agency, then either punishment is essentially wrong, or else, it rests upon some other consideration than Moral Agency. Having repudiated in toto the idea of Free Will, he next comes to the subject of the true reason for punishment.

But it is fated too, that he who doeth ill, shall suffer. And for this cause he doth it—that he may suffer what he suffereth, because he did it.

There is no evasion of the issue here. Hermes frankly admits that in every instance that a man does an evil deed, it was through the necessity of Fate that he did it, and that there was no way by which he could avoid the deed. He freely admits that there is no moral responsibility whatsoever attached to the commission of a sin, seeing that there is no way to avoid the commission of that sin, all sinners are sinners not from choice but from necessity. As there is no power of choice left to them, they are not morally guilty. But, while it is fated that the one who does the evil deed shall do the evil deed, the necessity of Fate rendering it quite impossible for him to escape its commission, yet, it is likewise decreed through the necessity of Fate that every one who does ill, although he had no power to keep from doing it, nevertheless he shall suffer for his sin. He goes on to say that man sins in order that he may suffer what he suffers for doing it. In other words, we sin in order that we may suffer the penalty of our sin. Fate compels a man to sin, giving him absolutely no choice in the matter, solely in order that He may inflict upon the man the suffering due for such acts. Man sins then, not of choice but of necessity, for no other reason than that he may suffer the penalty of his sin. This at first glance, looks as though an injustice were being committed by Fate. However this is not the case. We must realize the true mission of suffering. In the first place though, we must bear in mind that man is not punished in a legal sense for his sins. The evil deed, itself brings upon the sinner the suffering that is due for such evil deed. In other words, the necessity of Fate is such that the evil deed itself, necessitates the suffering which it brings upon the guilty soul. Suffering comes only as a result of evil deeds, and without evil deeds, one would not suffer. Were it not for suffering there would be no upward progress in the life of the soul. Through suffering, the gross condition of the soul is disintegrated, and it becomes more volitile, more effervescent, and hence capable of a much higher rate of vibration. The psyche is therefore refined and elevated through the suffering that afflicts the soul. The soul does evil, in order that it may suffer, and through suffering, it may become refined of all the grosser elements. Its suffering is, therefore, the means of its higher evolution, and it is for this reason that it sins, in order that through the suffering attendant upon all sin, it may be refined and thereby perfected. Suffering therefore, has a therapeutic action upon the soul, it is the healing medicine that cures the gross condition of the soul, and thereby, brings her into the status of the fine, highly evolved soul. This is the true mission of suffering, and the soul suffers, not as a punishment for choosing evil in preference to good, through an exercise of her power of choice, but as a medicine in order that the psyche of which she is composed may be transformed from evil to good, and through this chemical action of suffering upon the stuff of which she is made, she may become chemically a good soul instead of being chemically a bad soul. The problem of sin and suffering is, therefore, not a moral problem but a chemical problem. It is in fact a problem in Alchemy, and Suffering is the Alkahest that transforms the soul as the Matter of Art, and sin is the means of bringing the soul matter into contact with the Alkahest of suffering. Sin and the consequential suffering are in fact the Plan of Salvation for the soul, and they are in fact the dual aspects of the Grace of God to the human soul. It is from a recognition of this true mission of suffering that Asceticism has derived its greatest impetus. It is seen to be in perfect accord with the workings of Fate and with the transmutation of the soul from bad to good through suffering. And there is no doubt of the fact that if the pains inflicted through the ascetic practices can be made to act upon the soul, so as to inflict suffering upon her, they will be aids in the way of her purification and perfection, through the transmutation of her matter and of her nature.

6. But for the moment, [Tat,] let be the teaching (*logos*) as to vice and Fate, for we have spoken of these things in other [of our sermons]; but now our teaching (*logos*) is about the Mind:—what Mind can do, and how it is [so] different,—in men being such and such, and in irrational lives [so] changed; and [then] again that in irrational lives it is not of a beneficial nature, while that in men it quencheth out

the wrathful and the lustful elements.

Of men, again, we must class some as led by reason, and others as unreasoning.

But for the moment, Tat, let be the teaching (*logos*) as to vice and Fate, for we have spoken of these things in other [of our sermons]; but now our teaching (*logos*) is about the Mind:—what Mind can do, and how it is [so] different,—in men being such and such, and in irrational lives [so] changed; and [then] again that in irrational lives it is not of a beneficial nature, while that in men it quencheth out the wrathful and the lustful elements.

The present sermon deals primarily with the Mind, hence, what is stated in reference to vice and Fate is merely incidental, and enough has been said on that score. We must return to the discussion of the Mind as it is related to the life of the soul, whether it be the case of a human soul or the soul of an irrational animal. What has been said in regard to vice and Fate has been said in order that it might be shown that the teaching in regard to the function of the Mind is in no sense in conflict with the teaching in regard to Fate. The subject matter of the present sermon deals primarily with the Mind as to what It can do, or its function and powers, the differences in the workings of the Mind, and the way in which it differentiates the diverse souls of men the one from the other, and likewise in the changing of irrational lives the one from the other, and likewise from the types of human souls. In a word, we are to learn how it is that all diverse types are due to the action of Mind upon the soul. By this we do not mean the psychic individualities, but rather the grades and classes of souls, separated from each other in accordance with their relative values. It also shows how it is that the action of Mind in the case of the irrational animal souls is not

of a beneficial nature, seeing that it co-operates with
their natures, and thus, does not introduce any transformations in the natures of such souls. In other words,
in the case of the irrational lives, Mind is directed in its
action by the nature of the soul, instead of controlling
the soul, and causing it to evolve in harmony with the
Mind. To make the matter clearer, in such irrational
souls, the Mind is not the *Norm* governing the action of
the soul, but on the contrary, the Soul is the *Norm* to
which all the actions of the Mind conform. In the case
of men, the action of the Mind is such as to quench out
the wrathful and the lustful elements of the soul. This
quenching is after the manner of water quenching out a
fire, and hence the wrathful and lustful elements are
likened unto wrathful and lustful flames of fire. A
wrathful element is an element full of wrath, just as a
lustful element is an element full of lust. In the sense
in which the terms are used here, being full of wrath,
means an element, the quality of which is pure wrath,
while being full of lust, means an element, the quality of
which is pure lust. We have previously indicated the
nature of lust to be the strong, negative and centripetal
motion of the psyche, which draws into it, the energies
of the objects of sense, and in this way, forms within
the soul, their images, nourishing and strengthening them
within the depths of the psyche. This is the nature of
desire, and lust is merely a strengthening of the desires
until they dominate and control all the actions of the
soul. A lustful element of the soul, will be a portion of the psyche that is so completely acted upon
by the force of a particular lust, that no other
energy can act upon it, in this way, bringing that
portion of the soul stuff completely under the control
of the force of lust. It is thus, that through those lustful elements, the soul becomes merely the passive matter
in which the forces of lust play, being energized by the
images of sensibles. In a word, through these lustful

elements, the soul becomes merely the sensorium for the imaging of all the sensibles, possessing no power of direct action, but being able to do nothing but react to the stimuli of these sensibles, through their images that are resident within the soul herself. It is in this way that the lustful elements bring the soul into subjection to the sensibles, and thus, she is led captive by lust. We are assured that the action of the Mind in man has the effect of quenching out these lustful elements just as a flame of fire is quenched by water. It is through the dynamic action of the Mind upon the soul, that these centripetal currents are changed, and are made to act under the guidance of Mind, unto the end that the soul may express the Mind in all of her actions, and thus, the images of the thoughts of the Mind will take the place of those images of sensibles. By quenching the lustful elements, we are to understand that the Mind is to prevent the soul from imaging sensibles, and to force her to image intelligibles in lieu thereof. By preventing her from imaging the objects of sense, the Mind forces the soul into the higher state, and as a result, all the lustful elements are quenched out, and their place is taken by intelligible elements that are of the nature of the Mind. Just as lust is the centripetal force exercised by the images of sensibles, through which those images draw unto themselves the energies of sensibles and are thereby nourished, wrath is primarily the centrifugal force engendered by those images of sensibles, which darting forth from these images as centers of action, act as driving forces against whatever in the world without, will work against those images. They are the positive forces of the images of sensibles, that work destruction of whatever is not in harmony with them. Wrathful elements, are those portions of the psyche, completely energized by this force of wrath. Lust and wrath are, therefore, the centripetal and the centrifugal forces engendered by the images of sensibles, and hence the lustful and the wrathful elements will be the psyche, or soul stuff, completely energized and dominated by, the centripetal and the centrifugal forces of those same images of sensibles. The Mind quenches out the lustful and the wrathful elements of the soul, by reason of its powerful action upon the psyche, so as to dominate all of its vibrations, and thereby, to reduce it to a static condition, so that it becomes a body moved by the Mind, acting under the action of the Mind. In this way, the psyche, no longer acts under the centripetal and the centrifugal action of the Images of Sensibles, hence they become inactive, and their elements are taken from them, and are brought under the direction of the Mind. It is in this way that the Mind quenches out all of the wrathful and the lustful elements of the human soul. This is the work of Mind and of Mind alone, and thus it is that Mind exercises this beneficial influence upon the souls of men, which it does not do in the case of the souls of the irrational animals.

Of men, again, we must class some as led by reason, and others as unreasoning.

We have seen the distinction between man and the irrational lives to be that in the case of men, the action of the Mind upon the soul is to rid her of all the wrathful and the lustful elements, and to free her in this way from the dominion of the images of sensibles, and bring her into a condition where it will be possible for her to act under the guidance of Mind alone, while in the case of the animals, no such action is performed by Mind, which works in conjunction and in conformity with the nature of the animal soul. Bearing in mind this distinction between the action of Mind upon man and upon the irrational lives, we must now see in what way we are to class men as being differentiated the one from the other as to grade and class. We are told that the souls of men group themselves into two classes, and that all souls of

men belong to one or the other of these two classes.
These two classes of human souls are those led by reason,
and those who are unreasoning. This does not mean
that there are some who have Reason, and some who are
destitute of the Reason. A man devoid of the Reason
will not be a human soul, but an irrational animal soul.
It is the possession of the Reason that renders a soul
human, hence, without Reason one would not be a man.
The distinction here given, is between those souls that
are led by reason in all things, and those souls who do
not exercise their reason. Between souls that reason,
and souls that do not. By the latter, we are to understand those souls, whose psychic activities are the result
of the psychic reaction of the soul to sensations derived
from the world without. They are what we might term
the instinctives in contradistinction to the rationals. In
the case of the instinctives, all action springs from
impression, instinct and sensation. They form their
opinions, and act, from experience and observation, they
are *sensible* people, in the sense that all their actions
spring from the exercise of their senses. These instinctive people, act without the guidance of the reason, and
hence they are the creatures of impulse and feeling, their
souls reacting to external stimuli, which makes their
psychic life nothing more than the psychical reaction to
the sensations of the body. This leads to the condition
of the soul in reality being controlled by the body. On
the other hand, the rationals, are those persons who are
led by reason. Their conduct is determined not by *nature*
but by reason. Such people act from the standpoint of
thought not from natural impulse. They are never
sensible, for they never permit their senses to spontaneously produce actions, they are rational in all things,
seeing that their actions are determined by their reason.
In the case of the rational men, the reason determines
the psychic life to a great extent. We do not mean that
they are free from the psychical reactions of the soul to

the action of the senses, we mean that they form their
opinions, and determine their conduct on the basis of
reason, and not through impulse. In a word they control their impulses, and their instincts through the exercise of their reason, unto the end that, being led by
reason, and not by instinct and sensation, they may be
rational in all their actions, never sensible. This applies
to their psychic life entirely and to their physical life
to a very great extent. It is into these two classes of
rational souls, who are led by reason, and into instinctive souls, who are unreasoning, and hence are led by
nature and instinct, that all human souls are divided.

7. But all men are subject to Fate, and genesis
and change, for these are the beginning and the end
of Fate.

And though all men do suffer fated things, those
led by reason (those whom we said the Mind doth
guide) do not endure like suffering with the rest; but,
since they've freed themselves from viciousness, not
being bad, they do not suffer bad.

Tat. How meanest thou again, my father? Is not
the fornicator bad; the murderer bad; and [so with]
all the rest?

Her. [I mean not that;] but that the Mind-led
man, my son, though not a fornicator, will suffer just
as though he had committed fornication, and though
he be no murderer, as though he had committed
murder.

The quality of change he can no more escape than
that of genesis.

But it *is* possible for one who hath the Mind, to
free himself from vice.

But all men are subject to Fate, and genesis and
change, for these are the beginning and the end of
Fate.

While these two classes of men, the rational and the instinctive classes are differentiated as we have indicated above, yet all men are subject to Fate, the rational man being no more exempt from the determining action of Fate than the instinctive man. This is true because Fate is not related to the effects that the objects of sense may have upon the soul, or to the wrathful and lustful elements in the soul, nor yet to the action of the Mind upon the soul, but is entirely independent of the action of the reason. This working of Fate is related to a process over which the Mind, the reason, the will and the soul exercise no control; it is something connected with the composition of the soul itself. The beginning of Fate is in genesis, or the causing to be. Genesis is directly connected with *nature*. As we have previously indicated, *nature* is the process of perpetually being born, and hence is the center of creation, the creatorium as it were of our being. Genesis is the very root of *nature*, this it is which causes things to be born as being what they are. It is the creative side of nature, and likewise the generative aspect of *matter*, which is identical with the psyche when we are speaking of the soul. Fate, therefore, has its beginning in the very creatorium of the soul, and works through the genesis of the *nature* of the soul. All men must be subject to Fate, for the reason that they are of course subject to the genesis of their souls through their own nature. The end, or consummation of Fate is to be sought in change. This *change* is identical with transformation. This change is likewise the coming to maturity of all states generated, and their dissolution, and returning into the creatorium of genesis, as the germs of new states. Fate is that process which has its beginning in genesis, and its consummation in change, and is the expression of Becoming, through the inter-action of Life and Death, which is perpetually active in the psyche of every soul. It then is the process of Creative Evolution going on in the soul, and it works through the manifestation of the Law of Causation. It is this which determines the course which the life of the soul must pursue. Being, as it is, a process purely Chemical and Vital, there are of course no exceptions to the workings of this process. It is a process pertaining to psyche as such, and, therefore, in no sense effected by the question of whether the soul is guided by reason or not, neither is it influenced by the questions of the morality or immorality of the soul. All souls alike are subject to the workings of this process of genesis and change, and hence, all alike are subject to the rule of Fate, there being no exception from this Law and its workings.

And though all men do suffer fated things, those led by reason (those whom we said the Mind doth guide) do not endure like suffering with the rest; but, since they've freed themselves from viciousness, not being bad, they do not suffer bad.

All men therefore suffer those things that are fated by reason of the genesis and the change in their souls. There is no way by which anyone may escape the workings of this principle of causation within his soul. Yet is there a difference in the degree of suffering that falls to the lot of those led by reason, and the rest of mankind, who are the creatures of nature. Those led by reason are identical with those who are guided by the Mind. The guidance of the Mind causes men to exercise their reason, and thus, transcending the light of their nature, to free themselves from the force of nature. It is in this way that the leading of the reason, as a result of the guidance of the Mind, causes the rational class of humanity to escape the sufferings peculiar to the instinctive class of humanity. This is due to the fact that those who are led by reason, have through the exercise of their reason, and through the guidance of the Mind, freed themselves from all viciousness, inasmuch as they have shut out all of the vices that spring from the energizing of the soul by the senses, hence, being free from vices, they are not bad, seeing that the bad elements are not generated in their souls through the action of the vices, and thus, the bad is not present in such souls. And as they are not bad, they of course do not suffer the condition of being bad, nor do they pass through the sufferings that are caused to a soul by reason of the bad elements that are present in it. These bad elements are to be thought of as so many foreign substances that are present in the souls of the wicked, which act as so many poisons, to poison the soul, and thus cause those sufferings of the bad, which are in reality the pains of a poisoned soul. A soul that is led by reason does not contain these bad elements, and hence it is not poisoned by them, and as a result, there is nothing to cause it these pains that are the result of a poisoned soul, hence such a rational soul does not have to suffer bad, or the results of being or containing within it, bad.

Tat. How meanest thou again, my father? Is not the fornicator bad; the murderer bad; and [so with] all the rest?

Tat is confused by the foregoing teaching. He can think of badness as being nothing other than immoral deeds. To his mind, badness consists of such wicked deeds as fornication, murder and similar evil deeds. Now, he cannot think of any way by which the leading of the reason may of itself cause a man to refrain from fornication, murder and similar misdeeds: and if the reason will not prevent one from doing those wicked things, then, how can the leading of the reason keep a man from suffering the results of such bad deeds? He is judging man entirely by his conduct, instead of judging him by his being led by reason, or following the promptings of nature unguided by reason, which Hermes has shown to be the correct standard by which all men are

to be judged. We can easely see that Tat here represents the point of view of practically every one at the
present day, he is judging these matters from the Ethical
standpoint rather than from the Philosophical standpoint, which is the standpoint of Hermes. He has of
course missed the trend of the argument in the sermon.

Her. [I meant not that;] but that the Mind-led
man, my son, though not a fornicator, will suffer just
as though he had committed fornication, and though
he be no murderer, as though he had committed
murder.

What he means in this statement is, suffering is not
dependent upon evil doing. The man who is free from
fornication will suffer as though he were a fornicator,
and the man who has done no murder, will suffer the
same as though he were guilty of murder. He means
to teach that, contrary to the usual opinion, suffering is
not so much a penalty for sin, as a curative agency, and
every one will suffer, who needs the suffering as a means
unto his perfection. The whole theory of suffering that
Hermes is expounding is that suffering is a condition
growing out of certain transformations in the soul, and
that it is quite impossible for those transformations to
take place without the attendant suffering. In a word,
suffering is here looked upon as being in the nature of
a Chemical process, and it is believed that it is impossible for those chemical changes to take place in the composition of the soul, without the resultant suffering.

The quality of change he can no more escape than
that of genesis.

In this paragraph we learn why the Mind-led man
cannot escape from suffering. We are told that no one
can escape the quality of change, anymore than he can
the quality of genesis. As the diverse states are generated within the soul, so in like manner, they must all

reach their respective ends, and through change, disintegrate and return as the germs and seed of genesis. The psychic elements are generated through the action of genesis, and having reached their maturity of development, they must of necessity, disintegrate, that they may be formed again into new elements, for, otherwise the continual evolution and transformation of the elements of the soul could not be. This disintegration of the elements that they may become the seeds of genesis for new elements, is what is indicated here by change. The Mind-led man can no more escape the quality of such change, than he can the quality of genesis. Were he to escape the quality of change, there would be no seeds of genesis, and hence, the genesis of the soul would cease, and this would mean that her *nature* was at an end. As the soul's immortality depends upon this process of perpetual genesis, the cessation of this process of genesis, and hence of the *nature* of the soul, would mean the extinction of her immortality, and hence the soul would die. The continuity of the soul, therefore, depends upon genesis, and as genesis depends upon the seed of genesis, which come only as a result of change through dissolution, it follows that the continuity of the soul depends upon change. As change is a process of disintegration in the psychic elements of the soul, it will of course follow that this metamorphosis or transmutation in the elements of the soul, must of necessity be a very painful one. Suffering is the result of this transformation. As this transformation cannot result without suffering, it is quite impossible for any soul, no matter how thoroughly it may be led by the Mind, to escape this suffering, seeing that were it to escape suffering, it would cease to be transformed, and that would mean death. Suffering, is therefore, a fundamental condition of the life and growth of the soul. The suffering that is here spoken of then, is that suffering which is a condition of genesis and of change, that in fact, which is a condition of all trans-

formations, and hence of all growth, the growing-pains
of the soul we might say. This kind of suffering, no
soul can escape, it is common to all souls alike. From
this it will at once appear that there is no escape from
the suffering of the soul. It not only suffers while
incarnate in a physical body here on the physical plane,
and likewise, when it leaves the physical plane in death
and goes to the Spirit World, clothed in the Spirit, but
even when freed from the spirit, the soul goes on to
Heaven, she will still suffer, seeing that the root of
suffering is within herself and not an external condition.
All progress and evolution would cease, were she to
cease to suffer. Therefore, you had as well give up the
hope of escaping suffering even when you go to heaven.
Suffering can only cease with death, and that the death
of the soul. In this we see how perfectly correct was
the Buddha when he taught that only in the final extinction of Nirvana can one escape suffering.

But it *is* possible for one who hath the Mind to free
himself from vice.

While it is not possible for any one, the Mind-led man
included, to escape suffering, seeing that that is a condition bound up in the qaulity of genesis and change, and
hence, a fundamental quality of the soul as a soul. But,
while the man who has the Mind cannot escape this perfectly natural suffering, yet, through the guidance of
the Mind, it is possible for him to free himself from
vice. The real advantage of being led by the Mind is
not in the escaping of the suffering that is bound up in
the natural changes in the soul; but in the ability of
such a man to entirely free himself from vice. By this,
we are not to understand that all men led by the Mind
are free from vice, but simply that it is within the
possibility of such a man to free himself from vice,
something that is not possible for one who has not the
guidance of the Mind. By this we are to understand

that vice is perfectly natural for an instinctive man who is not led by reason, and that it is simply impossible for such a man to free himself from this condition until such time as he becomes guided by the reason. All men who follow the promptings of their own natures, their natural impulses, their feelings and their instincts, who are ruled by their sensations, all *sensible* men in fact, are fundamentally and naturally vicious. It is only when a man is led by reason, that he reaches the point where it is possible for him to free himself from vice, and lead a life of virtue instead of a life of vice. Virtue is, therefore, the quality of the rational man, who is led by reason. It is through the guidance of the Mind alone that any one is able to escape the net of vice and attain the status of virtue. Thus we are able to classify men as being rational and instinctive, and the instinctive men we are forced to class as the naturally vicious, while we will have to class the rational men as being those who have it in their power to free themselves from vice, through the exercise of reason. These rationals we may again divide into two classes, the rational man who has it in his power, ultimately to free himself from vice, and the Mental man, who has actually accomplished this work of freeing himself from vice, and who being free from vice, is at the present time, absolutely virtuous. Thus we will have three classes of men in this way. It may as well be stated at this time that vice here does not refer to the physical vices of the body but to the psychic vices of the soul. The vices of the soul are the result of the imaging of *sensibles* within her, and it is only through their eradication through the action of the Mind upon the soul, that the vices of the soul may be eradicated. This is accomplished through the imaging of *intelligibles* within the soul, unto the end that she may be filled with Cosmic Ideas and the Ideas of the Mind and Reason, as the *seed* and *germs* of her subsequent genesis.

LESSON IV.

MIND'S FATE.

8. Wherefore I've ever heard, my son, Good
Daimon also say—(and had He set it down in written words, He would have greatly helped the race of
men; for He alone, my son, doth truly, as the First-
born God, gazing upon all things, give voice to words
(*logoi*) divine)—yea, once I heard Him say:

"All things are one, and most of all the bodies
which the mind alone perceives. Our life is owing to
[God's] Energy and Power and Æon. His Mind is
Good, so is His Soul as well. And this being so, intelligible things know naught of separation. So,
then, Mind, being Ruler of all things, and being Soul
of God, can do whate'er it wills."

Wherefore I've ever heard, my son, Good Daimon
also say—(and had He set it down in written words,
He would have greatly helped the race of men; for
He alone, my son, doth truly, as the First-born God,
gazing upon all things, give voice to words (*logoi*)
divine)—yea, once I heard Him say:

We start out here with a saying of Good Daimon. As
this is something that Hermes has heard Good Daimon
say, it follows that it is in the nature of an Initiation
that this has been uttered. The statement that Hermes
has ever heard this, would suggest that it was in the
nature of a perpetual voice ringing in his ears, or a
logos ever present in the consciousness of Hermes, as being a definite part of the Fair Faith. As the authority

of the Good Daimon is to Hermes absolute, it will be
well for us to understand exactly what we are to understand by the Good Daimon, and to understand that we
must bear in mind that He will be of a nature similar to
that of other daimones, only He will be distinguished
from them as being Good which they are not, and also,
that while there are many Daimones, there is but the *one*
Good Daimon.   Daimones are used by Hermes in two
senses, first as the Sower of Seed, in the sense of the
impregnater of the Mind with the Seed of Thought, and
hence the husband of Mind and the father of thought,
and in the second place, as the Configurer of species.
The Good Daimon then will be the one who sows the
Good Seed of thought, or the Seeds that bring forth
Good Thoughts.   The Impregnator and the Fecundator
of the Mind with the Divine Seed of God, coming direct
from Ku or the Divine Essence.   In this sense, Good
Daimon is practically the same as the Sense of God
spoken of in the Sermon on Sense and Thought.   In the
sense of being the configurer of species, Good Daimon
will be that aspect of Divinity which causes all the Species in the highest and most ultimate sense to become
configured as what they are, the originator of species in
the most ultimate sense.   It is that which makes all
things to be what they are.   He is spoken of here as
being the First-born God, which can only mean that He is
the First to be born of the God beyond all Name, who is
the self-existent God, who as Mind and Ku, gives birth to
Good Daimon.   Good you will remember is the Esse
of God, being that and nothing else.   This being the case,
Good Daimon can be nothing other than this Esse of
God or Good acting as Daimon.   This will mean that
Good is acting as the Impregnator and the Fecundator
of Mind, as the Sower of the Seed of Thought coming
from God, Good as the Sense of God, hence, God functioning as God the Energizer.   Likewise, He is Good as
the Configurer of Species, the Artificer, Architect and

Creator of all things. He will also, as the First-born God, be the first Emanation from, and the First Differentiation of the Divine Principle in its highest sense. As He gazes upon all things it will follow that He is back of all things, and anterior to all things being in fact the Arche or Source of all. He is in fact the Mind in its highest sense, as being the Mind as the Essence of God in action as Energy. He is the Mind as the Thinker, and the Logos as the Speaker of First Words. This is what is meant by His giving voice to Divine logoi or words, that He is the Logos of God as well as the God Mind, and hence the Mind of the Good. This is why He is called the Good Daimon, and from this of course you can see at once that His authority must be beyond all question.

The quotation that follows this paragraph has puzzled a great many. This quotation appears to be an almost verbatim quotation from the sayings of Heracletus, and also in Section 1 and in Section 13. Now it appears that in three places in this Sermon, Hermes is quoting from the writings of Heracletus. At the same time, Hermes distinctly says that he has heard the Good Daimon say this, which would suggest that he was in no sense of the word quoting from any human authority. Again, Hermes says: "And had He set it down in written words, He would have greatly helped the race of men." The explanation given by G. R. S. Mead is far from satisfactory. To hold that it was not written simply because it was not written in books accessible to the people of the Tat grade of students, is in the opinion of the present writer, very far fetched indeed. There is here no mention of *publication,* but the regret that Good Daimon had not written in words this statement. By implication, Hermes states as positive as words can make it, that this quotation has *not* been set down in written words, that it has never been committed to writing by any one. There is but one satisfactory explanation for this statement, and that is, Hermes lived and taught before Heracletus was born. Hermes was not quoting Heracletus, but later on, Heracletus quoted Hermes. This was extant in the written books of Hermes previous to the time of Herecletus. The quotations that Mead gives, showing the similarity between Hermes and the Christian Gnostics simply go to show that at that time, the Books of Hermes were well known and were perused by all who laid any claim to philosophical scholarship, and were the basis of Gnosticism. The earliest form of the Gnosis is undoubtedly to be found in the books of Hermes, and it follows that the Heathen Gnostics were a Sect of Hermetics, and the Christian Gnostics being a branch of the Gnostics, their wisdom is traceable directly to the Hermetics. As the books of Hermes were accessible in written form in the days of Heracletus, it shows the great antiquity of the Hermetic Teachings, and greatly favors the tradition which places the date of the Fourth Hermes at thirty-five hundred years before Christ.

"All things are one, and most of all the bodies which the mind alone perceives. Our life is owing to [God's] Energy and Power and Æon. His mind is Good, so is His Soul as well. And this being so, intelligible things know naught of separation. So, then, Mind, being Ruler of all things, and being Soul of God, can do whate'er it wills."

The main purpose of this paragraph is to show the unity of all things. This unity in all things is in reality due to the unity in the bodies which the mind alone perceives, seeing that these are the intelligibles that are back of all the sensibles. This fundamental unity does not exist in sensibles, but it subsists in their intelligible arche-types. We are assured that our life is owing to

God's Energy and Power and Æon. It is through the inter-activity of the Energy, the Power and the Æon or Eternity of God that our life is rendered possible. In fact our life is the result of that combined action. God's Mind is stated to be Good, that is It is the Good Mind, and His Soul is likewise Good, seeing that it is of the very *essence* of God which is the same as being the *essence* of the Good. We are informed that Mind is the Soul of God. This is true, for we must distinguish between the Good Mind which is Mind of God and Mind which is His Soul. The Mind of God is the Ultimate Divine Mind which is Primordial, and constitutes the Fatherhood of God, just as Ku or the Good constitutes the Motherhood of God. This Mind of God is at all times working in conjunction with Ku or the Divine Esse, which receives all of the Thoughts of the God Mind, being impregnated thereby, and in Her turn, She makes after the pattern of those Thoughts of the God Mind. Therefore, the Mind of God is perpetually absorbed into the Divine Esse or Ku, so that as Mind of God, it is never able to escape. It is consumed as the Spermal Seed that impregnate the Womb of the Divine Motherhood, Who makes all the Ultimate Principles thereby. For further information on this line see Philosophia Hermetica and Scientifica Hermetica, where this mystery is explained in detail. The Mind of God is therefore in a state of perpetual coetus with Ku or the Motherhood of God, and through the Thoughts of God She is kept in a state of perpetual impregnation and fecundation, which causes Her to make all things as Monads. Mind as Soul of God is something *other* than the Mind of God, which is the *same* as the Fatherhood of God. Mind as Soul of God is the radiating Energy and the Active Essence of God. It is in fact the Common Mind that we have previously spoken of. But this Soul of God is also Good, from which we are to learn that the Mind itself is Good. By this we are to understand that as to its quality, Mind as Soul of God is the *same* as God and not *other* than God in quality. It is the Essence of the God Esse. Being the Activity of the Divine Passivity. Now, intelligible things are the direct productions of this Mind as Soul of God. They are the products of Mind and as such are superior to soul. In their production, Mind is Thinker, while Æon is Maker under the fecundation resulting from the thinking of the Mind. In this way are intelligibles produced as a result of the interactivity of Mind and Æon. They are therefore, superior to the Plane of Hyle and to Cosmos as well, though they themselves, constitute the very highest aspect of Cosmos. It is for this reason that intelligibles know naught of separation, seeing that they are of the *nature* of Mind and Æon if we might use such a term with reference to *them*. The Unity of God passes through the Mind into the intelligibles and becomes unity in them. For this reason, there is only unity, and never separation in the intelligibles. It is these intelligibles that are the bodies which the mind alone can perceive; for they are the Seeds, which through Sense enter into the mind and there impregnating the mind, cause it to conceive thoughts after their likeness, hence they can be conceived by the Sense of the Mind alone. They are too pure for the senses of the soul ever to perceive them. As they are the absolute unity, therefore, it is that this unity is perceptible to our mind alone. The unity in all other things is due to the fact that sensibles exist because of the generative power of their respective intelligibles. These are therefore the Ideas of all things, Ideas which we can deal with by the reason alone. Ideas being the intelligibles which are in fact the *forms* of the *thoughts* of the Mind. Mind, is the Ruler of all things, because it is the Mind that brings into being the intelligibles which are the Ideas of all things, and as the Ideas are controlled by the Mind, it follows that all things derive their *courses* and their respective *trend* from the Mind, *the*

norm of their being subsisting in Mind. Thus it is that
the Ideas which are the *determinatives* of all things are
ever fixed in Mind, thus it is that Mind is Ruler of all
things. As the Soul of God, Mind likewise gives to the
intelligibles not only their Idea but their Will, not only
their Light, but likewise their Life. Thus it is that
Mind can do whatever it wills to do. That is to say,
Mind, acting as Dynamic Force, is irresistible, being
creative in all of its movements, hence, whatever Mind
thinks, it does. Its thoughts are in all cases realized in
action. This is the power of the Creative Word, Mind
thinks the thought, Reason speaks the word, and it is
brought into realization in action. Of course it must be
borne in mind that we are here speaking of the Mind, in
the sense of the Soul of God, the essence of the Divinity,
hence the Universal Mind, not of the mind in man, which
is quite a different matter. At the same time, bear in
mind this, the mind of a man, is not distinct from the
Mind, it is not *other* than the Mind, it is the *same* as the
Mind, being differentiated quantitatively, but not qualita-
tively, hence that unity subsists between the mind in a
man, and the Common Mind, and hence between the
mind of one man and the mind of every other man. It
is in mind alone therefore, that men are all one. It is
in our mind that we are one with all and each. Through
this unity of our mind with the Mind, it is possible for
us to attain supreme power when we have learned to
function entirely in the Mind, to live in intelligibles and
not in sensibles. This is the Great Work in the Art of
Alchemy, but this is not the place to give instructions in
the correct formulae.

9. So do thou understand, and carry back this
word (*logos*) unto the question thou didst ask before,
—I mean about Mind's Fate.

For if thou dost with accuracy, son, eliminate [all]
captious arguments (*logoi*), thou wilt discover that

of very truth the Mind, the Soul of God, doth rule
o'er all—o'er Fate, and Law, and all things else; and
nothing is impossible to it,—neither o'er Fate to set
a human soul, nor under Fate to set [a soul] neglectful of what comes to pass. Let this so far suffice
from the Good Daimon's most good [words].

Tat. Yea, [words] divinely spoken, father mine,
truly and helpfully. But further still explain me
this.

So do thou understand, and carry back this word
(*logos*) unto the question thou didst ask before,—I
mean about Mind's Fate.

With the information given above, we are now able to
go back to the consideration of the previous question,
relative to Mind's Fate, or to the relation between the
action of Fate and the functioning of the Mind. Knowing the nature of the Mind and its relation to intelligibles, and the action which they have upon all things
sensible, we are in a position to examine the workings of
Fate in the light of the workings of the Mind.

For if thou dost with accuracy, son, eliminate [all]
captious arguments (*logoi*), thou wilt discover that
of very truth the Mind, the Soul of God, doth rule
o'er all—o'er Fate, and Law, and all things else; and
nothing is impossible to it,—neither o'er Fate to set
a human soul, nor under Fate to set [a soul] neglectful of what comes to pass. Let this so far suffice
from the Good Daimon's most good [words].

We are here requested to eliminate all captious arguments, and to bring the pure reason to bear upon the
problem set before us. This problem is the relation of
Mind to Fate. The Mind of which he is speaking here
is the Soul of God, hence the Mental Energy of God,
which he calls the Common Mind in this sermon. From

what has been indicated above, we can see at a glance that the Mind rules over all. This is true because in the Mind subsist the Ideas of all things, and as these Ideas are the intelligible principles of all things, which cause the sensibles to be what they are, it follows of necessity that what rules and directs the Ideas of the things, will direct the things themselves, seeing that their Ideas are their determinating principles. This being true, the Mind must of necessity direct all things through their Ideas. The Mind rules over Fate, because Fate is the term that is used to indicate that sequence of causation which caused it to be fated that certain results shall come into being from certain causes. Fate, in a word, is the result growing out of the train of causation. Fate is, therefore, the work of the Mind, seeing that it is the Idea that determines the course of Fate, seeing that all causative action has its beginning in corresponding Ideas. As these are the work of the mind, it will follow that Fate is but the course of action that springs from the Ideas of the Mind through the logoi of the Reason. Fate is itself but the effect of the action of the Mind, and for that reason, Fate itself is subject unto the Mind. All Laws are subject unto the Mind, because Laws are merely the quality of energy, the manner in which it operates in its workings, and all energy is directed by Mind. Laws are in fact, the diverse courses pursued by Fate, and as Fate is ruled by Mind, so must of necessity all Laws be subject unto the Rule of Mind. We hear much said as to the immutability of the Laws of Nature, the question is, just what do we mean by the Laws of Nature? Nature, as we have previously indicated, is the process of being born, the state of the ever becoming, the perpetual process of coming into being. It is used with reference to a tendency in Matter to generate new states and conditions, and likewise, with reference to this process while it is in action. This being the case, it is the equivalent of genesis as an inherent principle in matter. Now, if Nature be the same as genesis, the question is, on what does genesis depend? It depends upon energy acting in a given way upon matter, so as to generate after a given quality, the elements generated depending for their quality upon the quality of the action of energy upon matter, that is, upon the quality of the energizing of the matter. The two prime factors of genesis will therefore be, energy and matter. The Laws of Nature can be nothing else than the determinative forces acting upon matter in such a manner as to determine the quality of nature that will result from such action. The determining factors in all natura will therefore be, the quality of the energy that acts through matter in such a manner as to determine the quality of nature. These energies are determined and set in motion by Ideas, and as these are the products of the Mind, it will follow that all the Laws of Nature are determined and set in motion through the action of the Mind. This being true, the Laws of Nature will absolutely depend upon the action of the Mind, and hence they will be regulated by the Mind, therefore, the Mind rules over all the Laws of Nature. For this reason, Mind as the Creative Principle back of all things, bears rule over them, and likewise determines their quality and their course of action. There is nothing that does not find its root and source in Mind, hence there is nothing, undetermined by Mind. It is for this reason that there is nothing impossible to Mind, all things depending upon it, and it depending upon nothing, there is nothing to divert or interfere with its free operations. It is stated that it is not impossible for Mind to set a human soul over Fate. This means that it is quite within the range of possibility for Mind to render a human soul superior to Fate, which means superior to the sequence of causation. This will place him in a position where he is not only not influenced by the sequence of cause and effect, but where he is even superior to that sequence, and can alter the course of its operations. This can have but one meaning; the Mind functioning in such a man as his mind, may reach the point where it determines the course of causation, in the sense that the thoughts of such a man are themselves creative and causative. Through his thinking, he will determine the workings of energy, unto the end that the laws of his nature will be the expressions of his own thoughts, and the only causative process will be the causative operations of the energies set in motion by his own thinking. His thoughts will in fact determine all of the laws operative in and through his own *nature,* and in this way will his nature be the creation of his own thinking. Thus will he be rendered superior to his Fate or to Fate, seeing that his fate will be determined by his own thinking, will be in fact the creature of his thought. Thus it is that the Mind working through the mind of a human soul may set that soul over and above Fate.

A soul that is neglectful of what comes to pass, that is, a soul who fails to exercise his mind for the determining of his nature, and thus instead of determining the forces that will bring about his future, permits nature to have its way with him, is through the action of the Mind, placed under the workings of Fate. The difference is that, in the former case, the Mind works entirely through the mind of the man, in its contact with and action upon the man's nature; but in the latter case, the Mind works upon the *nature* of the man, through the energies which It has determined and set in motion, working upon them independent of the man's mind. Thus it is within the power of man, through the exercise of his mind, to determine the course of his Fate through the control of the operations of his nature; but the man that neglects to rule his nature through the action of his mind, he alone will be subject to the workings of the Laws of Nature and to Fate. Of course we are speaking here of the *nature* of the soul, what is stated here as to the ability of a man to free his nature from the influence of all Laws as well as of Fate, and bring it completely under the control of his own mind, has reference to the control of the nature of the soul, though it is possible to extend it into the lower aspects of his being. However, this should suffice at this time.

Tat. Yea, [words] divinely spoken, father mine, truly and helpfully. But further still explain me this.

Tat accepts the truth of the foregoing teaching, realizing its perfect truth, and realizing the way to apply it in the evolution of his own soul. This is the meaning of his saying that these words are full of help. It is not enough that he should be taught to understand this principle as a philosophical proposition, but he must be able through this knowledge to help himself in the development of his soul. His words indicate an understanding of this, and an appreciation of the fact that it is now for him through the exercise of the powers of his mind, to permit the full manifestation of the Mind in his own thought, and in this way to create his own Fate through the action of his mind. It must be realized at once that he understands this to be the problem presented to him by his father, and that so far as the principles enunciated are concerned he understands how it is to be done. At the same time, he realizes there are certain difficulties in the way, and he now seeks a means of overcoming these difficulties. This is the meaning of his request for further explanations in the matter. We will find that his questions present the most serious obstacles in the way of the successful practice of the Art of Alchemy.

LESSON V.

ACTION AND PASSION.

10. Thou said'st that Mind in lives irrational worked in them as [their] nature, co-working with their impulses.

But impulses of lives irrational, as I do think, are passions.

Now if the Mind co-worketh with [these] impulses, and if the impulses of [lives] irrational be passions, then is Mind also passion, taking its colour from the passions.

Her. Well put, my son! Thou questionest right nobly, and it is just that I as well should answer [nobly].

Thou said'st that Mind in lives irrational worked in them as [their] nature, co-working with their impulses.

Having grasped the meaning of the teaching that has been given in regard to Fate and Mind, there are certain difficulties that occur to Tat. The divinity of Mind has been stated by Hermes, and it all looks clear from the point of view of the teaching that he has just been listening to, but now, the mind of Tat harks back to the previous instruction, touching the subject of the action of Mind upon irrational lives. This difficulty is found in the fact that, notwithstanding the greatness of the Mind, nevertheless, in the case of irrational animals, the Mind works in them as their nature, hence, in their case, there is nothing transcendent about the Mind, it is not something above their nature, ruling and directing their nature, but rather it is identical with their nature. This seems to be in conflict with the recent teaching on the subject of the divinity of the Mind. If in the animals, Mind is identical with their nature, then if Mind be divine, it would seem to follow that the nature of the animals would be Divine, which is something not to be thought of. Likewise, in the case of the irrational animals, Mind co-works with their impulses, and this would seem to indicate that the divine Mind is capable of harmonizing with the impulses of the animal nature. This would imply that those impulses themselves were divine, or else it would seem to indicate that Mind was not in all cases divine. The problem is to reconcile the divinity of Mind with its becoming the nature of an animal, and working in connection with his impulses, how are we to reconcile this apparent contradiction?

But impulses of lives irrational, as I do think, are passion.

These impulses in the cases of the irrational lives are identical with the passions, therefore, the problem resolves itself into the Mind co-working with the passions of the animals, and if Mind can work in connection with the passions, then, there can be no great inharmony between the Mind and the animal passions, hence, is the Mind of the nature of passion? If so, the Mind being divine, and being of the nature of passion, then of necessity, the passions are divine. If the passions are not divine, and the Mind is of the nature of the passions, then is the Mind not of the nature of divinity, and hence the teaching in regard to the Mind being the Soul of God, is of course wrong. The question is, how to solve this question aright.

Now if the Mind co-worketh with [these] impulses, and if the impulses of [lives] irrational be passions, then is Mind also passion, taking its colour from the passions.

His line of reasoning becomes syllogistic. His first premise being that the Mind co-works with these animal impulses. Seeing that the Mind co-works with them, it must be near enough to their nature to be able to work in unity with them. His second premise is that the impulses of irrational animals are passions. From these two premises he reaches the conclusion that the Mind itself is passion. If the Mind co-works with impulses that are in themselves passions, then the Mind is a co-worker with the passions, and as there can be no co-working between two antagonistic elements, it will follow that the Mind must be of the nature of passion, hence the Mind must itself be passion. This being true, the Mind will take its colour from the passions, that is to say, the quality of the Mind will be determined by the passions with which it works, and hence, the quality of Mind will depend upon the quality of the passions. This can only mean that the Mind is subject to the passions, and not superior to them. This description of the Mind is not at all in harmony with the description of the Mind which has been given when it has been spoken of as the very Soul of God, therefore, how are we to reconcile this apparent contradiction as to the true character and function of the Mind?

Her. Well put, my Son! Thou questionest right nobly, and it is just that I as well should answer [nobly].

Hermes admits the justice of all of Tat's conclusions, and hence admits that the Mind is passion. There has been no mistake in the matter, it is merely a failure to go deep enough into the examination of the question. What follows is, therefore, to be understood as being in the nature of an explanation of how the Mind is passion, and yet, to show that the passional nature of the Mind does not in any way detract from its essential divinity, how it can be both Soul of God and passion at one and the same time. The difficulty is that Tat has been a Dualist all the time, and hence has been unable to see the problem as being other than that of a Dual division of all things into the Essential and the Passional Realms with a sharp line of demarcation drawn between the two. To his mind, for Mind to be both Soul of God and passion at one and the same time is out of the question. His difficulty is identical with that of all other Dualists, the Pan-monism of Hermes is for him out of the question. In what follows, Hermes undertakes to make him understand this pan-monistic view of all things.

11. All things incorporal when in a body are subject unto passion, and in the proper sense they are [themselves] all passions.

For every thing that moves [another] is incorporal; while every thing that's moved is body.

Incorporals are further moved by Mind, and movement's passion.

Both, then, are subject unto passion—both mover and the moved, the former being ruler and the latter ruled.

But when a man hath freed himself from body, then is he also freed from passion.

But, more precisely, son, naught is impassible, but all are passible.

Yet passion differeth from passibility; for that the one is active, while the other's passive.

Incorporals moreover act upon themselves, for either they are motionless or they are moved; but whichsoe'er it be, it's passion.

But bodies are invariably acted on, and therefore are they passible.

Do not, then, let terms trouble thee; action and passion are both the selfsame thing. To use the fairer sounding term, however, does no harm.

All things incorporal when in a body are subject unto passion, and in the proper sense they are [themselves] all passions.

By things incorporal he of course means things that are not incorporated, that is to say, things not organized, or compounded, things which are in the body, not as other bodies, but as simply energies or forces. All things incorporal then will mean all forces which are acting in the body as forces and energies. There is a difference between the action of these forces when they are freed from bodies, and when they are operating in bodies. The term, things incorporal when applied to bodies, refers to those forces which are capable of subsisting outside of bodies in a free condition, which however enter into bodies, and there, become the energies acting upon and within such bodies, giving to them life and motion. They are the dynamic forces that acting upon the bodies cause them to move, through the motion which they impart to them. We are assured that all such incorporal things, when in a body, are there subject unto passion, and are in the proper sense of the word, themselves passions. This means that in the proper sense of the word, a passion is identical with an incorporal force or energy, acting upon a body.

For every thing that moves [another] is incorporal; while every thing that's moved is body.

This will enable us the better to understand the Hermetic use of the terms incorporal and body. With Hermes, a body is a mass of matter, destitute of the power of self-movement, one that has within itself, no power of movement, but one that can be moved by some other force. Any moveable body is called a body. It need not be a body of any particular kind of matter, it is a body so long as it is moved by force other than itself. A body then is anything that is moved. In like manner, that which acts as the motive power of a body, is itself, not a body, but an incorporal force. Things are incorporal because they move bodies, while other things are bodies because they are moved by something else. Call to mind the doctrine in Scientifica Hermetica about movement, giving the three factors of movement as the Mover, the Moved and the Space in which all motion transpires. All bodies are movable objects, and are to be classed as the Moved, while all incorporal things are to be classed as Movers. This moving is accomplished by reason of the incorporal Movers being present within the bodies to be Moved, so that acting upon them from within, and working in conjunction with the same energies without, they are able to move the bodies. Bear in mind then, that the incorporal refers to all forces present in bodies, and capable of moving those bodies by acting upon them as energies, while bodies are masses of matter that can only move as they are acted upon, and thereby, moved by the incorporal energies resident within them.

Incorporals are further moved by Mind, and movement's passion.

While incorporals move all bodies, in the sense of composed bodies, they themselves are moved by Mind, and hence are in the nature of bodies being moved by the energy of Mind. This will enable us to understand the usage of the term bodies, when applied to that which is certainly incorporal, in that case a body simply means a mass, deriving its motion from the Mind as the mover. These incorporals are in the nature of currents of moving force, the initial movement of which is derived from the Mind. The Mind then is the prime Mover that sets the incorporals in motion. It is the continual action of the Mind upon incorporal nature that causes these incorporal forces to be in motion, and they in turn acting upon bodies, move them. All movement then originates in Mind, the incorporals are merely the continuation of that movement through the incorporal forces of nature as well as of matter. All movement is passion, and hence, all incorporals being moved by Mind, and movement being identical with passion, it follows that, all passion originates in the Mind.

Both, then, are subject unto passion—both mover and the moved, the former being ruler and the latter ruled.

As movement is identical with passion, it follows that the mover is subject unto passion, seeing that it is through passion that it moves whatever is to be moved, and likewise, the moved is also subject unto passion, seeing that it is through passion that it is moved. The passion of the mover, rules the moved, seeing that through the motion given to it, the moved obeys the mover, so it is that the moved is ruled by the passion of the mover. Thus it is that it is through the passion of the Mind that the incorporals are moved and hence ruled, and in the last analysis all bodies are ruled and moved by the passion of the Mind. But, as the Mind moves all things by its passions, it is subject unto those possions, seeing that without such passions it could not move any thing, this renders the Mind subject to its own passions in so far, as it is under the necessity of moving things incorporal. In a word, the rule of the Mind over the incorporals is through the exercise of its passions, hence it is under the necessity of expressing those passions in order that it may rule, and being subject to the necessity of ruling all incorporal things, it is therefore subject to the necessity of having those passions, and thus is the Mind subject unto its own passions. All incorporals are subject unto the passions of the Mind, being but the continuation in motion of the passions of the Mind, being what we might say is the movement of the Mind's passions. This is particularly true of the movement in connection with the body. So long as there are bodies, they must be moved, and bodies cannot be moved without movement, and as all movement is passion, there can be no movement without passion, hence nothing can be moved without passion, hence there must be passion so long as there are bodies to be moved through the expression of passion.

But when a man hath freed himself from body, then is he also freed from passion.

When man is freed from the body he is freed from passion, because he has no corporal body to be moved, hence there is now no longer any necessity for the incorporals to move it, and being endowed with mind, his soul is moved by his mind, hence, there is needed no power outside of himself to move him, he is now able to live from his own center, where all is movement without anything to be moved, as he is neither moved himself, nor does he move any thing, he is, therefore, freed from movement and hence is he freed from passion. From this we can see at a glance that there is no such thing as freedom from passion so long as man functions in the body. It is not a question of being a good or a bad man, it is a question of having a body, that binds man in subjection to the passions, and one is freed from the passions only when he is freed from the body. This being freed from the body does not refer to the passing out of the body at death, but to the state of having transcended all bodily existence, so that a man passes out of the body for the last time, never to reincarnate again, having transcended the state of existence in a body. It is then only that he is made free from passion.

But, more precisely, son, naught is impassible, but all are passible.

By passible he means being subject unto motion, something that can be moved by reason of the action of some moving force apart from itself. The impassible would be that which could not be moved, that which was not subject unto motion by any force whatsoever. He means to say that there is nothing really impassible, that is, nothing immovable, but that all things are capable of being moved, hence all things are subject unto motion by some force incorporal in comparison with it. This being the case, and motion being identical with passion, it follows that there is nothing entirely free from passion, but rather, all things are subject unto passion.

Yet passion differeth from possibility; for that the one is active, while the other's passive.

Passibility is used with reference to the quality of bodies which permits them to be moved. The passibility of body is simply its ability to be moved. It is the passibility of a body that constitutes it the *moved*, that enables it to be acted upon by the motive force, and in this way permits its movement. Passibility is therefore, the term used to indicate the passivity of a body in the face of movement, that passive quality, which renders it passive under the action of the forces that will move it. Passion is the active force, that acting upon a passive body, causes it to move. It is the dynamic quality of force which enables it to move all passible bodies, that is, bodies that are passive under its action. It is the passion of a force that constitutes it the *mover* giving to it the quality which enables it to move the passible body. The passion of a force is therefore the measure of its capacity to move bodies which are passible, in the sense of being subject unto motion or movement. Just as we measure bodies by weight, thus indicating the force that is required to lift them, so does the passion of a force measure the mass of corporal matter that it will move. The passibility of the body is the ease with which it can be moved, and its impassibility is the measure of passion

that is required to move it. The passion of a force is
the degree of its activity upon a body, by which it is able
to move that body, and the passibility of a body is the
degree of its passivity under the action of force, enabling it thereby to be moved.

Incorporals moreover act upon themselves, for
either they are motionless or they are moved; but
whichsoe'er it be, it's passion.

Incorporals differ from corporals in that in corporal
bodies, the only action is that which incorporal forces
exercise upon them, but they themselves are purely
passible, but devoid of all passion, but incorporals, not
only act upon all corporal bodies, and are acted upon
by Mind, but likewise they act upon each other, and likewise do they act upon themselves. Incorporals are to be
divided into two classes, the motionless and the moved.
By motionless incorporals we are to understand those
incorporal forces which are expanded over a field and do
not move through space, they are not moved from one
part of space to another, but preserve their fixed local-
ity, though they are acted upon, and thus are energized.
Within them, energy is generated, which passing out
from them, energizes bodies with which it comes in contact, though these incorporal bodies if we may call them
such do not move with the energy which they send forth.
The moved incorporals are those that, being acted upon
by some other force are moved from one point in space
to another, and being moved, act upon bodies with which
they are brought in contact. But, it makes no difference
whether they are motionless or are moved, in either case,
it is their passion that enables them to act upon bodies,
and likewise, it is their passion that prevents them from
being moved, for impassibility does not depend upon
mere inertia, for that is in the very nature of passibility,
impassibility is the result of passion, or motive power
within, which prevents the incorporal bodies from being

acted upon, and thereby, being moved through the action of other forces. In proportion to the passion of incorporal bodies, are they impassible to the passion of other incorporal bodies, and the less passion there may be in a body of this kind, the more passible it will be to the passion of other bodies incorporal. Therefore, motionless bodies are such because of their passion, while movable bodies are movable because of the passion of the bodies that move them. It will be observed that we are speaking here of incorporal bodies, not of corporal bodies. Thus all movement depends upon the passion of the mover, acting upon the passibility of the moved, and in this way is the mover able to move the moved.

But bodies are invariably acted on, and therefore are they passible.

A body may be acted on in proportion to the degree of its passibility. The passibility of a body being the quality by which it is capable of being acted on. The bodies here spoken of are corporal bodies, and as they are invariably acted on, by the incorporal forces, it follows that these bodies are passible, seeing that it is by reason of their passibility that the incorporal forces are able to act upon them. Just as bodies are acted on by reason of their passibility, so do the incorporal forces, by reason of their passion, act upon bodies, through their passibility. Thus, all corporal bodies are seen to be passive in relation to incorporals, while all incorporals are active in relation to all bodies. The passibility of a body is then its ability to be acted upon by incorporal forces, and the passion of an incorporal force is its capacity for acting upon passible bodies.

Do not, then, let terms trouble thee; action and passion are both the selfsame thing. To use the fairer sounding term, however, does no harm.

Passion is, therefore, merely that quality of action that

enables action to move a passible body. This being true, all corporal bodiees are passible, while all incorporals are both passible under the passion of Mind and likewise are they possessed of passion when it comes to moving passible bodies. The Mind is, therefore, endowed with passion in that it moves all incorporals, though the Mind is not passible, in that there is nothing capable of moving the Mind itself. All this being true, passion is inherent in the Mind which is at the same time the Soul of God. In every instance, the passions are the active forces that move all things. Our dynamic power depends absolutely upon the strength of our passions. It is a mistake to assume that a man is bad in proportion to the strength of his passions, he is bad in proportion as he is acted upon by either his own passions, or those of another, that is, that part of him is bad that is moved by passion, seeing that the essence of bad lies in passibility. The essence of good lies in the power of passion, for the measure of strength and dynamic power is to be determined by the strength and irresistibility of the passions. The perfect man is the one in whom the entire being is determined absolutely and completely governed by the passions of the mind, which is itself the perfect expression in passion of the Common Mind. Let a man, therefore, not deplore the strength of his passions, but rather let him glory in them, for through them is he able to act upon bodies, his own and others as well; but rather let him deplore the fact that his passions are weak, and thereby, is he subject to the influence of others, being acted upon by the passions of others. Passion originating in the Mind which is the soul of God, it follows that passion is an attribute of the Soul of God, and hence partakes of the Divine Essence, hence passion is next to mind and reason, the most divine quality that we possess. In this way does Hermes show that while the Mind manifests through the passions, yet, this is not in conflict with its character as the Soul of God.

LESSON VI.

VOICE AND SPEECH.

12. *Tat.* Most clearly has thou, father mine, set forth the teaching (*logos*).

Her. Consider this as well, my son; that these two things God hath bestowed on man beyond all mortal lives—both mind and speech (*logos*) equal to immortality. He hath the mind for knowing God and uttered speech (*logos*) for eulogy of Him.
And if one useth these for what he ought, he'll differ not a whit from the immortals. Nay, rather, on departing from the body, he will be guided by the twain unto the Choir of Gods and Blessed Ones.

Tat. Most clearly hast thou, father mine, set forth the teaching (*logos*).

Tat is satisfied with the instruction of Hermes, which has shown how the Mind is passion and at the same time divine. The explanation has driven all trace of Dualism from his mind, and now Tat is able to see the Panmonism of the teaching. He now understands how it is that Mind can work as the nature of the irrational lives, and at the same time can rule the nature in the case of man, how all passion must find its place in the Mind. What is still more important, it is made clear, how in the case of human souls, the mind works through the passions, and thus controls the body, and therefore, how the middle line can be sought between a life of passion and a life of mind, not as a compromise in which the

(96)

two will be mixed, but rather as a state where they will
work together as one, mind as the *mover*, the passions
as the motive forces, the soul as the place of their action,
the space through which they act, and the body as the
thing moved, so that in all their diversity of action, they
will all operate as one Unity. This is doubtless the most
important part of the demonstration which Hermes has
given. It shows a way by which all of our passions may
be made use of as instruments of the mind, and hence
as aids in the transmutation of the soul, and in the regeneration of the body.

Her. Consider this as well, my son; that these two
things God hath bestowed on man beyond all mortal
lives—both mind and speech (*logos*) equal to immortality. He hath the mind for knowing God and uttered speech (*logos*) for eulogy of Him.

The two gifts of God that distinguish man above all
other mortal lives are mind and speech. The other mortal lives, that is, the animals have all of the other characteristics that man has, only in the possession of mind
and speech is he distinguished from the irrational lives.
As we have indicated before, the Mind functions in the
animals, but not as a mind, in their case it operates in
them as their *nature* not as individualized mind; but in
man, the Mind is individualized as a human mind. It is
the mind and speech that renders man, who is of mortal
life, yet equal to the immortals, for mind and speech are
immortal gifts. In the gift of mind, man partakes of the
essence of God, for the Mind is the Soul of God, and the
mind of man is nothing else than the Mind functioning
in him as his mind, hence, it is the Soul of God over-
shadowing and permeating his soul, so that through the
mind is man's soul joined to the Soul of God. It is in
this way that man partakes of immortality, not as an attribute of his soul, but as the result of his mind being
one with the Mind. Then, the immortality of a man is

through his mind. The function of the mind in man is to know God. Man is provided with a mind in order that, through its unity with the Mind, he may know God. The vast majority will impiously assert that it is not within the range of possibility for man to know God. This impiety is, however, the result of their ignorance of the true function of the mind. As the mind of a man is merely the Common Mind in connection with his soul, that portion of the Common Mind which he has individualized that it may overshadow his soul, and as this mind of his, possesses no activity of its own, but merely the individualized activity of the Common Mind, it follows that the activities of the Common Mind are reproduced in the mind of man. This will mean that the operations of the Common Mind are likewise operating in the mind of man, and hence, the mind of man thinks what the Common Mind thinks, the thinking being individualized to be sure, but, nevertheless, it is the same thought that is conceived in the mind of man, that is conceived in the Common Mind. This being true, the mind of man will have the same consciousness that the Common Mind has, hence, the mind of a man will know what the Common Mind knows, that and nothing else. Now, the Common Mind is nothing else than the Soul of God, being the very essence of God in radiation, the radiating energy of God as we have previously shown. It is God in action, and the purest and finest as well as the first emanation from God Himself. God the Mind is in reality Mind as Principle, and Mind as the *process of thinking,* while Ku, the Motherhood, is God as Esse and as the Substance through which this *Thought* of God in the sense of the *act of thinking* acts, and likewise is She the process of *making;* but the Mind is the Mind of God in the sense of the sum total of the *Thoughts of God.* From this, it will be seen that there can never be in the Common Mind any thought which is not the absolute thought of God Himself. These thoughts of the Mind, act upon the mind of a man as Seed of Thought, for through Sense, God sews them in the particular minds that will receive them, through the Sense of the human mind, they are received, and are planted as *seed* in the *soil* of the mind, or as the *spermal seed* in the matrix of the mind, which as a result of such impregnation conceives thoughts after their image and likeness. Thus, while the mind of man is not as to its thinking exactly the *same* as the Common Mind, neither is it in its thinking *other* than the Common Mind. Because in this way is God conceived in the *mind* of man, and hence abides in man's mind, it is possible for man to know God. This is what is in reality meant by a man's conception of God, it is conceiving of God within his mind that is meant. A man can know God because he *conceives* God in his own mind. By conception of God we mean *conception* as the result of the impregnation of the matrix of the mind by the Seed of God. We mean sexual conception in every sense of the word. Now, we are assured that man has the mind simply in order that he may know God. This statement means much more than it appears to mean on its surface. We have shown that the mind knows God, because it conceives God in it as a matrix, that it is the Mind sewing Seed of Thought in the mind of a man, which mind, as a matrix, conceives thought from the Seed thus sewn by the Common Mind, which enables the mind of a man to conceive God. This is the way the mind knows God by conceiving God in this way. Now, this being the way that the mind knows God, it will follow that in as much as mind is given to man in order that he may know God, it follows that man has been provided with mind simply in order that he may in his mind *conceive* God as we have indicated above. He has a mind in order that the Mind as Soul of God, may through the Sense of God, sew in this mind the Seed of Thought, and thereby impregnating the matrix of the mind with these Seed of Thought from God, cause the mind to conceive thoughts of a similar character. Thus the Mind in man is the avenue through which God is manifested in the man. The mind is, therefore, given to man, that through its action, God may be reproduced in man, and thus each man may become a manifestation of God. This is the true function of the mind in man, and it is this that makes him equal to immortality, seeing that through the mind, and this way of knowing God, man is able to manifest God while still in his mortal flesh.

The other immortal gift is said to be uttered speech. It will require some explanation to enable you to understand the meaning of his statement that uttered speech is an immortal gift, and particularly, the statement that it is given to man for the purpose of eulogy of God. It will be observed that uttered speech is here called logos. This term, logos, is used either for a discourse, an instruction, a sermon, a doctrine, a word or for the reason, and also the universal Reason is called the Logos. Logos is likewise the term of the Word, in the sense of the manifest Word of God, and also for the Reason of God. As we have stated before, the mind conceives all thoughts, but in order that a thought conceived in the mind may become a force, it must be uttered, and the uttering of a thought is the function of the reason. In man, it is the function of the reason to clothe the thoughts of the mind, and in this way, develop them into ideas. The idea being the form of the thought. It is the form of the thought, the idea as the image of the thought, not in the sense of being something apart from the thought, used to represent the thought, but rather, in the sense of being the image created by the thought, the pure image which the thought itself creates, and through which it lives, the image in the sense of being the vehicle of the thought. At the same time, this form is above the plane of soul, being supernal in its composition. It is in fact the substantial form of the thought.

As such, it is individual, and likewise possesses within itself, the forces and energies peculiar to it. The reason gives to its ideas their individuality, and in this way, establishes their differentiations the one from the other, and likewise, links them together in their comparative relations. All thoughts of the mind are one, but the ideas of the reason are diverse. Words are said to be the signs of ideas, and in the highest sense of the word, they are nothing else than ideas vehicled in sound. Modern language has become so complicated that it is difficult to understand the relation of ideas to words, but if we go back far enough into the foundation of language we will find the fixed relation of words to ideas. It is well known that Ideographic Language preceded Phonetic Language, and for this reason, we will have to go back into the period of Ideographic language to find the identity of words and ideas. This means that we must reach back to a point where one word is not derived from another, but where all words are distinct. This means a period where there is absolutely no grammar, no separate parts of speech, and where all words are nouns, that is, names of things. Now, in this primitive stage of language, we will find that the words which are used for naming things, will be the words that will name the primary impression of the thing, which the senses give to the consciousness of the speakers. For instance, we will say that the name for the Duck will be the Quacker, because he is associated with the quacking sound which he makes, the monkey will be the chatterer, and the Crane might be called the Wader. The point which I wish to bring out is that the names of things, are those names which recall to the mind of man, the impression which the sight or hearing or other senses of man have given to his mind. In a word, primitive man named not the things themselves, but his ideas of them, and their names were used to recall those ideas of things to mind once more. Words, therefore, are not so

much the names of things, as the names of man's ideas
of the things which they name. It will therefore be seen
that words are not only the signs of ideas, but that in the
primitive stages of language they are the utterance of
man's ideas of things. In almost all languages, the word
for man means the thinker, which indicates that primitive
man associated man with thinking, and that his idea of
a man was the idea of one engaged in the act of thinking. What phonetic language may have done in the
derivation of words and languages does not affect the
question of the origins of the first words. If words have
been derived, they must have been derived from words
previously existing, and we must recede to the point
where the words were underived. This will ultimately
lead us to the point where the words were merely the
names for the ideas suggested by things, and by association of the idea of the thing, with the thing itself, names
of the things. This leads us to the consideration of
Typology. A type is a thing, the idea of which is associated with an abstract idea. Typology is, therefore, the
science by which abstract ideas are communicated
through the medium of the ideas of things. Man is the
thing that thinks, hence the idea of man is the same as
the idea of the thinker, and hence with the act of thinking. This leads man to become the type of thought as an
abstract idea. What is called picture writing soon leads
up to a reproduction of this system of typology. Ideographs are the signs chosen as the means of communi-
cating the idea of a thing which one man has to the consciousness of another man: Ideographs are, therefore,
the means by which ideas are communicated in writing.
In the ideographic stage of spoken language words are
the spoken ideographs which likewise communicate ideas
of things. Hieroglyphics are a system by which the
ideas of things are associated with the abstract ideas to
which they correspond, and these abstract ideas are represented in writing, but in such a way that we will know

that they are the ideographs of abstract ideas, and not of things.

All this goes to demonstrate that words are in their purest form, the expression through the medium of sound, of ideas that are back of them. When a word first comes into existence, it is the natural expression of an idea, by the natural expression we mean that the nature of the idea has expressed itself in the word, that the idea has generated the word. The reason must formulate the idea, and this in turn must energize the vocal organs in order that they may express the word which is the manifestation of that idea through the medium of the voice. A word is then, an uttered idea, words being the utterance of ideas. An unuttered word is an idea conceived in the mind as a thought, given a form as an idea by the reason, and uttered by the reason, but not as yet voiced as so much speech. Speech is merely the vocal utterance of ideas. All words have their origin in the reason. Of course, there is the difficulty here of words becoming conventional. When words have been conventionalized, they become the regular vehicles of ideas, and their use molds the thoughts and idea of those who use them, thus it is that a language invariably transforms the thought of the people who use it. This is the way in which words become *thought-forms,* being literally the forms which the thoughts of the people take, and likewise the molds which give form to the ideas and thoughts of the people. This will enable us to understand how uttered speech comes to be an immortal gift. It is the means by which the ideas of the reason are rendered living, dynamic forces. Ordinary speech is merely the ghost of the speech that is here indicated. This speech is not merely the speaking with the vocal organs, it is the speaking with the reason. The reason speaks when words spontaneously flow from the ideas of the reason, and are in fact the utterance of the ideas. Such words, and such words only, are *logoi*. A logos in the sense of a discourse is a discourse which comes directly from the reason. Uttered speech has been conferred upon man for eulogy of God, because when the mind has conceived God through the instrumentality of God thoughts, the reason clothes this thought of God as the idea of God, these God thoughts as God ideas and utters them as God words, making the God idea to appear as God talk. This is why God Words lose their power when put in books. Through uttered speech in the way that we have indicated, it is quite possible for one to express the ideas of the reason in terms of vocal force. In this way can the Image of God conceived in the mind, and clothed in the reason as the Form of God or Idea of God, be uttered by the voice as a Divine Voice, and made to live in the form of uttered speech. To make our meaning clearer it may be stated that the Seed of Thought from the Mind, entering the mind of a man, and there conceiving thoughts, are in this way transmuted into human mind-stuff. These are through the action of the reason, given form, thus being transmuted again, and through the action of the reason, they are uttered as logoi, which means their transmutation into modes of Sound Force, what the Hindus call Fohat. These acting as active energies, or passions, energize the psyche of the soul, where they are transmuted into activities of the Sonoriferous Ether of the soul, which are reproduced or transmuted into spirit, and then into physical ether, after which, acting as passions, they move the vocal organs of the body, which are passible to them, and in this way are we able to give audible utterance on the physical plane to the very thoughts conceived in our minds by reason of the impregnation of the mind by the Seed of Thought from the Common Mind. It is for this reason that uttered speech is an immortal gift, and also it is for this reason that it is said to be given to us for eulogy of God, it is in fact the transmutation of the knowledge of God into speech. Of course this is quite *other* than the speech of the average man. This is the true meaning of Godly Conversation, it is conversation made up of Mind-engendered words. A man speaking the Word of God simply means a man whose words are uttered by the reason from the mind, the seed of which thoughts come from the Common Mind.

And if one useth these for what he ought, he'll differ not a whit from the immortals. Nay, rather, on departing from the body, he will be guided by the twain unto the Choir of Gods and Blessed Ones.

Here we learn that it is not every one that uses the mind and uttered speech as he should, that is, for the knowledge and eulogizing of God. As a matter of fact very few men do. Nevertheless, if one does use them for this purpose, for the knowledge and the eulogizing of God, he will be in no sense different from the immortals. Using his mind in the identical same way that the immortal gods use their minds, he will have the same kind of a mind that they have, differing in no sense from them as to his mind. By using his reason in the same way that they use their reason, he will have a reason precisely the same as theirs, and hence he will differ from the gods in no sense so far as his reason is concerned. And as his soul is energized by the same kind of *words* that energize the souls of the immortal gods, the result will be that it will be transmuted the same as are their souls, so that in essence, and in action, his soul will be the same kind of a soul as are the souls of the immortal gods. His mortality will then be confined to his spirit and his body. For this reason, when he departs from the body, and sheds the spirit, and as a soul takes flight, he will be of the same *nature* as are the immortal gods, likewise of their essence, and for that reason, guided by his mind and uttered speech, by his thought and words, he will come to the Choir of Gods and Blessed Ones. This means that he will become a part of that Choir, being counted with the number of the Blessed Ones and as a Companion of the Gods, seeing that he is of their own nature and essence, and that his passions are the same as are their passions, his passibility identical with their passibility. This is the glorious destiny of those men who think with the mind impregnated by the Seed of Thought form the Common Mind, and who speak from the ideas of their own reason. Of course this does not at all apply to the wicked, the ignorant and the superstitious. We are speaking not of the Natural Man, but of the Artistic Man, the man self-regenerated through the Art of Alchemy. This is the destiny of the Rational and the Mental Man, not of the instinctive and impulsive man.

13. *Tat.* Why, father mine!—do not the other lives make use of speech (*logos*)?

Her. Nay, son; but use of voice; speech is far different from voice. For speech is general among all men, while voice doth differ in each class of living thing.

Tat. But with men also, father mine, according to each race, speech differs.

Her. Yea, son, but man is one; so also speech is one and is interpreted, and it is found the same in Egypt, and in Persia, and in Greece.

Thou seemest, son, to be in ignorance of Reason's (*Logos*) worth and greatness. For that the Blessed God, Good Daimon, hath declared:

"Soul is in Body, Mind in Soul; but Reason (*Logos*) is in Mind, and Mind in God; and God is Father of [all] these."

Tat. Why, father mine!—do not the other lives make use of speech (*logos*)?

The question brought out here is the use of speech by the animals. The character of speech by humans has been indicated, and it is with some surprise that Tat hears it stated that articulate speech is something peculiar to the human soul alone. He assumes that the animals speak the same as do men. For this reason it is clear to us that he has not grasped the true nature of speech as it has been indicated by Hermes, the fact that speech comes from the reason, that articulate speech is identical with the utterance of the ideas of the reason in terms of sound. This point, words as the vocal expression of ideas, being the very essence of speech, shows that only those who reason, can possibly speak. It is this identity of ideas and words, as the prime element of speech that he has not understood, and it is for this reason that he is surprised that speech is limited to the human beings, and is not participated in by the animals. By his using the term *logos* to indicate speech, he seems to think that the animals utter ideas, that they speak words as the audible expression of ideas, and this would of course indicate that he thinks that these animals make use of reason at least in a small degree.

Her. Nay, son; but use of voice; speech is far different from voice. For speech is general among all men, while voice doth differ in each class of living things.

Speech is peculiar to humanity alone. None but the human beings make use of speech. What other lives make use of is voice. We are informed that speech is general among all men, while voice is found to differ in each class of living thing. In other words, each class of living things has its own peculiar voice, there being no unity in the voices of the different classes of living things. Thus, we can tell to what class any animal belongs by reason of the voice it uses. On the other hand, the speech of the human race is the same. There being no distinction in the speech of humanity, for all men use the same speech. It has been previously shown that speech is the utterance of ideas, words being merely ideas manifesting through sound. The statement that all men make use of the same speech, simply means that all men give utterance to their ideas when they speak. This being the case, the words uttered must of necessity be, those words which are the manifestation through sound of the ideas which they have. There can be no other form of speech than this utterance of the ideas. Thus all men use the same speech, for the reason that they are uttering their ideas. The ideas being the forms which the reason gives to the thoughts of the mind, it will follow that their speech can only express the action of the reason, and hence, their speech will be nothing other than the manifestation of the reason through the medium of sound. Now, the reason is able to operate in only one way, it must discriminate and classify, all the thoughts of the mind, clothing them in such a form as to permit their correct manifestation. While it is individualized, nevertheless, the reason in all men, follows the same plan, and as there is a common action of the reason in all men, it will follow that the ideas will be formed in accordance with a common principle of action, hence, ideas are common to all men, and are of the same character. This being true, there will be an unity in the speech of all men, because of the unity in the ideas of all men. As the reason embodies the thoughts and thus makes them to live as ideas, and as there is an unity in this action on the part of the reason in all men, it will follow that the real seat of unity or differentiation in speech will have to be sought in the mind. However, as the mind in a man is identical in essence with the Common Mind, it will follow that it must act in the same way that the Common Mind acts. Seeing that the mind in man is the matrix which being impregnated with the Seed of Thought from the Common Mind as Soul of

God, conceives thoughts after the image and likeness of
the Seed which cause the mind to conceive them, it will,
of course, follow that the thoughts will present an unity,
identical with the unity present in the Common Mind.
This will mean that all thoughts must in the very nature
of things be general to all men, there being no distinction to be drawn between the thoughts of one man and
those of another, save merely the slight transformation
which the individualized state of the mind-stuff will
cause. At least there will be no distinction between the
thoughts of one class of men, and those of another, the
only differences being in the case of individual minds
and their thoughts. The same kind of thoughts then are
general to all men, hence no difference can be found so
far as the thoughts go. Now, the reason in man, is an
expression of the Reason or Logos in the same sense that
the Mind in man is an expression of the Common Mind,
that is to say, the reason in man is merely an individualized form of the General Reason of the whole Intelligible Cosmos. The modus operandi of the human reason
is determined by the action of the Cosmic Reason, and
hence, the action of the reason in giving form to the
thoughts will be similar to the action of the General Reason in giving form to the Thoughts of the Common
Mind, and thus transmuting them into the forces of
Cosmic evolution. As this is one, it will follow that the
action of the human reason will be an unity of action,
and for this reason, all words must be the same, seeing
that the speech of all men as to the speech of the reason
must be the same. From this, it follows that the same
unity that is preserved in the mind and the reason because of the unity of the Common Mind and the General Reason, must also be present in the speech of all
men, seeing that their articulate speech must be the same
as that of the Logos through Fohat or the principle of
sound. Of course there is room here for individual pe-
culiarities owing to the individualized state of the mind

and reason in man, but that does not alter the fact that all men speak the same words having the same speech, because they think the same thoughts, and their reason gives to their thoughts the same ideal forms, embodying them in the same way and after the same rational mold. Thus it is to be seen that while voice differs in each class of living thing, nevertheless human speech is the same in all men, there being no varieties of speech, and men all use the same words in their speech. Of course, it is essential that you should bear in mind the definition which we have given as to the meaning of words and speech. With this in view, there is but the one speech among all mankind.

Tat. But with men also, father mine, according to each race, speech differs.

In this statement, Tat brings up the question of the diversity of languages. We have learned how all men have the same speech, but Tat confounds speech with language, and calls to the attention of Hermes the fact that the diverse races have their own peculiar languages, and so he assumes that this is in conflict with the theory that language is but one. This unity of speech suggests the unity of language, and so Tat assumes that if there are diverse races speaking diverse languages this shows that human speech is diverse and not one.

Her. Yea, son, but man is one; so also speech is one and is interpreted, and it is found the same in Egypt, and in Persia, and in Greece.

While Hermes admits the diversity of languages, he still insists that speech is one. Man is one, that is, there is an unity of mind, and an unity of reason in all men. Thus, the thoughts and the ideas of all men are the same, seeing that the human mind is but the Common Mind working into the human soul, and the same is true of the working of the General Reason working into the soul

as the individual reason of the man. This assures an
unity of thought and of ideas, in the case of all men. As
all men have the same thoughts and ideas, it will follow
that they will have the same *thought-forms,* and hence,
they will utter the same speech, that is, their thought-
forms will find audible utterance as the same words, thus
all men will make use of the same words, and hence
speech must of necessity be one. This could not be otherwise, seeing that it is the reason that speaks, that the
ideas are manifesting as words, and that all men have
the same ideas. He goes on to say that speech is interpreted, so that it is the same in Egypt, and in Persia
and in Greece. By this he means that the Egyptian
words have their equivalents in Persian and in Greek,
and so with all of the other languages. The fact that
the words of one language can be interpreted in such a
manner as to be understood by those speaking another
language, shows that the words of one language can be
transformed into the words of another language. This
can only mean that the ideas of Egyptians, Persians and
Greeks are the same. There are racial differences in
the forms of words, but not in ideas, for all ideas are
the same. For this reason, the ideas of one people can
be communicated to the reason of another people, seeing that they are all the same ideas. There are no distinctions between the ideas of one race and those of
another. The translation of a word, is merely the changing of the Persian name of that idea to the Greek name
of the same idea. In order to translate a word from one
language into another, we must first reduce the word
back into the idea which it expresses, and having done
that, we give it the form which it has in the language
which we wish to speak. Were it not for this unity of
ideas, the interpretation of words into another language
would be utterly impossible. At the same time it may be
contended that this does not mean the unity of words
and speech. It may be held that this in itself grants

that a Greek word is different from a Persian word. But this is exactly where you will be wrong. There is no such thing as a Greek word, a Persian word, or an Egyptian word, there are only words, and they are the same among all peoples. A word as we have previously shown is nothing else than an idea expressing itself through sound, and as all ideas are the same among all peoples, it must of necessity follow that all words are identical no matter what language we take up. It is not possible to coin a new word, unless you are able to have an idea that no one else has ever had, and to give expression to that idea. Languages differ from each other, not in any difference in their words, but in the different forms which they give to the words which they all make use of. The linguistic differentiation is in the peculiar form that has been given to words, and the translation of a word from one language to another, is simply a matter of changing the form of that word until it takes another form, but it is still the same word all the time. The forms which words assume in the languages of the diverse races will be seen to depend largely upon the stage of physical development of those diverse races. Language will be seen to start in Clicks, from the clicking stage it will pass into Gutturals, from the guttural stage into Nasals, and from the nasal stage into the condition of Palatals, Dentals and Linguals, and when the lingual, dental and palatal stage has been reached, Clicks, Gutturals and Nasals will have almost entirely disappeared from the language of the people. Now, these changes are due to physical changes in the organs of articulation, and are purely physical. It is of course true that these physical differences are largely due to psychic differences in the souls of the people. Yet, the differences are in all cases, differences in the form of the word, never in the word itself. Of course, when the language passes from the Ideographic to the Phonetic stage there is a much more rapid change in the transfor-

mation of the language. But it is because the same
words assume a diversity of forms in the diverse languages that the science of Comparative Philology is possible. Also the science of Comparative Etymology shows
that the derivation of words follows a definite law, which
is applicable to all languages alike. When we have understood Comparative Syntax this matter will become
clearer yet. Philologists are coming to realize that
Philology is not the study of languages, but the study of
language as one. This will become yet clearer as we
learn more and more languages. Reduce any number of
phonetic languages to the original ideographic stage,
and you will see that they are fundamentally the same
language. Of course, due allowance must be made for
the influence of the conventionalization of the language,
and for the influence of having to use the conventionalized form of a word as the means of expressing that
word in conversation. Phonetic decay is an element that
must be given its full credit in this transformation of
language. Take notice that when we speak of the transformation of language, we simply mean the changing of
the form of the word to some other form, but in every
case leave the word itself intact. Likewise, translating a
word from Greek into Zend merely means changing the
form of the word from the Greek form to the Zend form
of the same word, but the word itself is not effected, it
only changes its form. The major difference in the
formation of words in the diverse languages is the effect
of the senses upon the soul. Owing to the fact that difference in environment, presents different objects to the
senses of the people, and as a result, those sense-engendered ideas, which are the result of the imaging of the
sensations of sensibles in the soul, will of course, be different. These sense-engendered ideas may confuse the
consciousness so that it will not be able to consciously
realize the ideas of the reason, and hence a difference in
viewpoint will arise, and likewise language will be ef-

fected in its form. At the same time it must be borne in mind that all people who are guided by the reason, have the same ideas and use words in the same sense. Thus it will be seen that differences in language are not differences in speech, but merely in the form of that speech which is itself one, and differences in the forms of words, though in no sense different in the words themselves which are eternal and unchangeable. Enough, however, has been said here with reference to speech and language. We have shown that just as thought is one, and reason and hence ideation one, and as man is one, so speech is one, and unchangeable, for it is the logos in action.

Thou seemest, son, to be in ignorance of Reason's (*Logos*) worth and greatness. For that the Blessed God, Good Daimon, hath declared:

The difficulty with Tat is that he is ignorant of the worth and greatness of the Reason, in the sense of the Universal Logos. He makes the mistake that every one else does, that speech is a human invention, or else, the result of the evolution of man from the animal stage. There are those who think that human speech has evolved to its present diversity and perfection as the natural result of man's evolution from the monkey, and that all human speech has evolved out of the chattering of the monkeys. If this theory was true in regard to the development of human speech, it would be unthinkable that this unity of speech could possibly be brought about. Human speech is not the result of the evolution of man. It is the expression of the Logos through the reason of man. Tat is in ignorance first, of the fact that speech is in reality the speaking of the Logos through man, and second, of the worth and greatness of the Logos. Were he to understand this, he would at once see the divinity of human speech, and would realize that it is nothing else than a divine and immortal power, function-

ing through man, rather than a product of the man himself. We are now introduced to a quotation from the
Good Daimon. By the Good Daimon declaring this, we
should understand that what He declares, is in reality
a condition which He has established, that this connection of the Principles is one that has been established by
the action of the Good Daimon, in the sense of his being
the fabricator of that connection. This being the case,
the relation of the Principles is absolute and divine, and
nothing could ever change it a particle.

"Soul is in Body, Mind in Soul; but Reason
(*Logos*) is in Mind, and Mind in God; and God is
Father of [all] these."

Mind forever subsists in God, in the sense that Mind
is merely the radiating energy of God, an energy that is
the very essence of God, for this reason, the root of Mind
is in God, as Mind is merely the active energy of God,
radiating forth from God, hence it is the continuation of
God as active energy. While Mind is in God in the sense
of energy radiating *from* God, it is in Soul in the sense
of energy entering *into* Soul. It is a light shining out of
God, and shining into Soul, thus it is the Centrifugal
Energy of God, but Centripetal Energy energizing Soul.
Soul is perpetually energized by Mind, so that Mind is
that energy that unites Soul with God. God is Energizer, Mind is the Energy of the Energizer, and Soul is
the thing Energized by Mind. Soul is Passibility, Mind
is Passion, and God is the Actor. In this way are God,
Mind and Soul connected. Reason or *Logos* is in Mind
also, but in a different manner to what Mind is in God
or in Soul. Reason is an aspect of the same force as
Mind, and yet it is in such a way as to change the nature
of the force. We have previously shown the function
of Reason to be the giving of form to thoughts, by
clothing them with substance, so as to make of them
Ideas, the embodying of them as ideas, in this way, they

are differentiated into classes by the action of the Reason. Of course the Reason has its other function, which is the discriminative, but this is also a process of classification, for it is through this act of discrimination that the Reason *determines* the class to which any idea shall belong. Also, through this act of discrimination, the Reason determines the entire course of evolution in the Soul, and hence of all the world below. It is this discriminative action of the Reason, that particularizes all life, and in this way is relativity brought into being. Again, it is the Reason that prevents the Mind from being acted upon by the world of Sensibles. In a word, the Reason is the Guard on the line of demarcation between the Intelligible world and the Sensible World. In this way, Reason prevents Intelligibles from being acted upon by Sensibles, and directs the action of Intelligibles upon Sensibles. It is in this way that Reason is centered in Mind, and thus through Mind, God, Reason and Soul are all united in one, that is Mind. We have the Trinity then of God, Reason, and Soul, and one is their essence, Mind. This does not mean that Psyche is the same essence as Mind, but rather that it is the Mind as Energy acting upon Soul that determines the manner of her action, that Soul is energized by Mind, and hence Mind is the energy of Soul. God is Father of all these in the sense that we have indicated. They are all manifestations of the energy of God, hence they are all His productions without the introduction of any other element. Of course all that has been said here about the Principles, God, Mind, Reason and Soul, apply to the Common Mind, to the Cosmic Reason, and to the Universal Soul in their relation to God. At the same time, bear in mind that the mind of man is but the individualized portion of the Common Mind in conjunction with his soul, not separated but one with the Common Mind. Likewise the reason in man, is simply the Reason in connection with the Mind, both energizing his soul, and thus is man likewise one with the Common Mind, the Cosmic Reason, the Universal Soul and God. Thus, all that has been said here applies also to man. This we trust will enable you to understand the connection here, and then you will see how badly mistaken Tat was, and also how far are those from the truth, who assume that man has developed his own powers, instead of merely manifesting that which comes from God. Of course, what we say of the transcendency of man applies to the pious man who is guided by Mind and piloted by Reason, the wicked who are under the dominion of the senses are not partakers of this great glory of man. However, this will be more perfectly developed as we go on in our study of the sermon. It is only the rational and mind-led man that is in constant communion with God through his upper realm, the rest are cut off from intelligibles by the dominion of sensibles.

LESSON VII.

Cosmic Alchemy.

14. The Reason, then, is the Mind's image, and Mind God's [image]; while Body is [the image] of the Form; and Form [the image] of the Soul.

The subtlest part of Matter is, then, Air; of Air, Soul; of Soul, Mind; and of Mind, God.

And God surroundeth all and permeateth all; while Mind surroundeth Soul, Soul Air, Air Matter.

Necessity and Providence and Nature are instruments of Cosmos and of Matter's ordering; while of intelligible things each is Essence, and Sameness is their Essence.

But of the Bodies of the Cosmos each is many; for through possessing Sameness, [these] composed Bodies, though they do change from one into another of themselves, do natheless ever keep the incorruption of their Sameness.

The Reason, then, is the Mind's image, and Mind God's [image]; while Body is [the image] of the Form; and Form [the image] of the Soul.

We are told that the Reason is the Mind's image. We are of course to understand that this has reference to the Common Mind and to the Cosmic Reason or Logos. Image is here used with reference to the Fiat or impression of a Die or Stamp. It has the meaning of a reflection with the added element of permanency. The imaging of something in another substance, after the man-

(118)

ner of the negative and the positive in photography. By
saying that the Reason is the image of the Mind, he
means to say that the Reason is merely the result of the
action of the Mind playing upon the surface or within
the depths of *Substance,* and there producing within that
substance a form of action, which is the exact reproduction of its own action. We then, have Mind acting upon
passible substance, which as a result of such action, is
thereby energized, so as to reproduce this action of Mind,
the action of this substance being merely the reproduction of the action of Mind. In this way is Mind imaged
in Reason, the Mental process of thinking, being imaged
in the Rational process of Ideation. It is thus that the
action of the Reason is the image of the Mind. The
Mind is God's image in the same way. The Mind being
the radiating energy, in which the activity of God is reproduced. In this way is God imaged or reproduced in
the Mind. The Form spoken of here is the Spirit, and
this is stated to be the image of the Soul. Do not confuse this statement of the principles with the arrangement of the Principles in man, we are dealing here with
the Universal Principles. It is the Universal Soul that
is imaged in the General or World Spirit. The Soul in
this arrangement is active, and its passions, or activities, acting upon the possibility of the Spirit or Form,
image the Soul in the Spirit, so that the Spirit is the
Form of the Soul, the Form in the sense of being a Form
in which the activity of the Soul is imaged, thus all the
activities of the Soul are reproduced in the Spirit Form
so that it becomes the Fiat of the Soul. In the same way,
is the Spirit Form imaged in the Body of the Universe.
The action of the Spirit upon physical matter, transforms it, through its possibility, so as to make of it, the
physical image of the Spirit Form, just as the Form is
the Spiritual Image of the Soul. The Spirit is the Form
to the Body, because it is this Spirit Form that determines the construction of the Body. The Body is what

it is because of the imaging of the Spirit in physical matter, and likewise the Spirit Form is what it is because of the imaging of the Soul in Spiritual Matter or Air, that is Pneuma or Spirit. Thus the Body is passible to the passion of the Spirit, the Spirit is passible to the passion of the Soul. It is in this way that this sequence of imaging goes on. Each one of these Principles is in reality the image of the one above and within it. In this way is all Nature merely the sequence of imaging from the image of God down, hence all life is the action of God imaged into lower states of being.

The subtlest part of Matter is, then, Air; of Air, Soul; of Soul, Mind; and of Mind, God.

Not only is it true that the diverse Principles are imaged in each other, but it is also true that they are so perfectly united, that they are joined together, the one being vehicled in the other. This is why we are told that the subtlest part of Matter is Air. Air as used in this connection means Spirit, or Pneuma, while Matter in this sense is of course the Physical Matter of which bodies are composed. We are told that there is in reality no sharp line of demarcation between the Spirit and Matter, but rather the Spirit has entered into Matter, and so united to it, as to become the subtlest part of physical matter, so that it is difficult to determine where Spirit ceases, and Matter begins. In the same way, Psyche or Soul enters into Spirit or Pneuma, blending with it, and becoming the subtlest part of Spirit. Mind, likewise, enters into Psyche or Soul, uniting with it in such a way as to become the subtlest energy of Psyche or Soul. And God enters into Mind and is the subtlest part of Mind. God energizes Mind, Mind energizes Soul, Soul energizes Spirit and Spirit energizes Matter. Mind is the vehicle of God, Soul the vehicle of Mind, Spirit the vehicle of Soul, and Body the vehicle of Spirit. In this way are all the Principles merged the one into the other. We are speaking not of the Principles in man, but of the Cosmic arrangement of the Principles. Mind is the receptacle for all the energies of God, Soul is the receptacle for all the energies of Mind, Spirit is the receptacle for all the energies of Soul, and Matter is the receptacle for all the energies of Spirit. Mind is full of God, Soul is full of Mind, Spirit is full of Soul and Matter is full of Spirit. Mind is the Pleroma of God, Soul is the Pleroma of Mind, Spirit is the Pleroma of Soul, and Matter is the Pleroma of Spirit. God acts in Mind, Mind is acted upon by God and acts upon Soul, soul is acted upon by Mind and acts upon Spirit, Spirit is acted upon by Soul and acts upon Matter, and Matter is subject to the action of Spirit.

And God surroundeth all and permeateth all; while Mind surroundeth Soul, Soul Air, Air Matter.

God is here spoken of as an Energy surrounding every thing. This energy in a state of universal diffusion is the true state of God. We must not think of God as a Center, or as an organism, those who think of God as a Personality or a body have entirely misunderstood the essence of God. As we have previously shown, God is two-fold, a Mind and an Esse. As Esse God is Ku. God as Mind and God as Esse are not two Gods but one God. Ku or the Divine Esse is the essential womb which is ever receiving the Thoughts of the Divine Mind, all of these God Thoughts are received by the Divine Womb of Ku or Divine Esse, and retained there. In this way is the totality of the Divine Esse in a state of perpetual impregnation and fecundation by all of the Thoughts of the Divine Mind. In this sense, Mind is the Fatherhood and Ku the Motherhood of Divinity, and all of both is in a state of perpetual coetus. This, mind you, is to be thought of not as in the nature of a personal embrace between two personalities, but rather as being in the nature of the perfect union between an Active Force and a

Passive Force to such an extent as to render them one Force. Owing to this, we find that there is no limit or boundary to the extension of this God Esse, but it is in fact that which is back of, and superior to all space. All that is, must therefore, be within the space filled by this Divine Esse; for as all things are the product of this God Esse, which is their Beness, they must of necessity, be within this God Esse. Thus it is that God surroundeth all things. Likewise is it true that God permeateth all things. Ku not only gives birth to all things, but She likewise energizes all things, seeing that it is Her activity that enters into the forms which She has Borne and acting as energies within them, thereby, energizes them. God must thereby permeate all in order that in this way all may be energized by God. At the same time it should be understood that it is only the Mind that God directly permeates and energizes, and likewise in the surrounding of all, it is only the Mind that God contacts, the energizing of all other things on the part of God is through the medium of the Mind.

In just the same way, does the Mind surround and permeate the Soul, using Soul here of course in the sense of the Universal Soul or Psyche. Soul is permeated by Mind, which acts upon and through Soul, energizing Soul. Soul is passible to the passion of the Mind. Just as God contacts Mind directly, so does Mind directly and immediately contact Soul. Because of the action of God upon the Mind, is the Mind able to act as It does upon Soul. Just as God subsists in the action of the God Mind upon the Ku Esse, and thus in their inter-activity is there life, so does the Mind radiate forth as the Essence of God. Ku is God as Esse while Mind is God as Essence. Thus Mind is both the Essence of Ku, and likewise, Her active Energy. Mind acts upon Soul as the permeating Energy of Soul, and likewise as the force surrounding Soul. In this way does the passion or action of Mind determine all of the movements of Soul through the passibility of Soul to the action of Mind. In the same way does Soul as Psyche completely surround and permeate Air or Pneuma, that is to say, Spirit. Soul permeates Spirit, and acting upon and within it, energizes the Spirit, so as to cause its action in all cases. Likewise does Air or Spirit, surround Matter and permeate it, acting both upon the surface of Matter and likewise upon its interior, so that Spirit energizes Matter both from without and also within, thus presenting the perfect sequence of action and transformation through energizing from God down to Matter.

Necessity and Providence and Nature are instruments of Cosmos and of Matter's ordering; while of intelligible things each is Essence, and Sameness is their Essence.

Necessity is another name for Fate. It is the determinative factor in the transformations of Matter in accordance with the principle of Causation. Providence is used with reference to that determinative factor of Cosmic transformation which is the in-working of Mind into the psychic side of Cosmic transformation. Necessity is used with reference to the material determinative process, while the determinative action of Mind is called Providence, because, being the action of Mind, it tends to lift the Cosmic operations above the stage of evolution which Necessity will bring them into. We might therefore, call Necessity Material Causation, and Providence Mental Causation. Nature we have previously explained. It is of course the process of being born, of coming into being through genesis. This being true, the statement that Necessity and Providence and Nature are instruments of Cosmos and of Matter's ordering means that the three instruments through which Cosmos orders Matter, that is, establishes the order in

Matter that we find, are Necessitv, or Material Causation, Providence or Mental Causation, that is, the causative action of the Mind upon Matter, and the process of Genesis through which all things are brought to Birth. We might also say that Providence is the action of Mind on Soul, Necessity the action of Spirit on Soul and Nature the inherent potency for Genesis, present in Soul. Matter then is acted upon by the three transformative actions of Providence, Necessity and Nature, and in this way is the order preserved in the transmutations of Matter preserved, and this Order in Matter is what goes to constitute and perpetuate the Cosmos. All the intelligible things are an Essence. Sensibles are bodies, but intelligibles are Essences. The Essence of these intelligible essences is Sameness. From this we learn that differentiation is not to be found in intelligibles but only in sensibles. This of course is inevitable, seeing that all intelligibles are the product of Mind and Reason, hence they must preserve their fixed unity in Mind and Reason. As all Intelligibles have the same Essence, and as they are but expressions of that one Essence, they are, therefore, one in Essence, hence there are not in reality Essences, but only Essence which is one. Thus is Unity preserved absolutely in the Intelligible Realm of Life, only is Sameness departed from in the Sensible Cosmos.

But of the Bodies of the Cosmos each is many; for through possessing Sameness, [these] composed Bodies, though they do change from one into another of themselves, do natheless ever keep the incorruption of their Sameness.

We now pass from the Intelligible Realm into the realm of the Sensible Cosmos. Needless to say, the first aspect of the Sensible Cosmos will be the Soul World. While it is true that the Soul World is the true realm of Time in the sense of Periodicity, nevertheless we may

term it the highest aspect of the Sensible Cosmos, seeing that all the Psychic Bodies are sensible to the Psychic Senses, though not to the Spiritual or the Physical
Senses. Now, a Body is of necessity different from an
Essence, and hence, seeing that all Intelligibles are Essences, it follows that all Bodies must of necessity be
Sensibles. These Bodies of the Cosmos are very nearly
identical with the Elements of the Cosmos. These are
not single Bodies, for it is distinctly stated that of these
Bodies each is Many. This can only mean that these
Bodies are to be thought of, not as organic bodies, but
rather as Elemental Stuff. They are, therefore, in reality the psychic elements, presenting themselves as
masses of the psyche. Their possession of Sameness
means that the identity of their elemental constitution
is never changed, but they are ever the same element.
They are called Bodies, only because they are Masses of
Psyche that are acted upon by the Intelligible Essences
acting as energies, thus it is the passibility of these Elements to the action of Intelligible Essences that constitutes them Bodies. These Bodies or Elements, go to
make up a great number of bodies, each class of these
bodies being composed of the same Element or Body as
we have previously spoken of. Owing to the fact that a
number of these bodies are composed of the same Psychic
Element, they change from one into the other. It is
through this process of metamorphosis that the evolution of psychic bodies is brought about. Now, while the
bodies of these Elemental Bodies change from one into
another of the same Elemental Body, yet the Bodies or
Elements forever preserve the incorruptibility of their
Sameness. Thus it is, that there is never any new Elemental Bodies in this Psychic World, yet is it true that
the bodies are ever changing and thus do they evolve.
The Sameness of the Bodies or Elements being determined by the Sameness of the Essences of the Intelligibles. These Psychic Bodies are composed of only one

Element, hence they are Simple Bodies, and their Essence as well as their Nature is Sameness, hence they must ever remain the *Same* as what they are, having in themselves not the power to ever become *other* than what they are. The bodies composed of these Elemental Bodies are likewise merely so many stages of this Element which composes them, hence they never lose their Sameness, but ever remain the *same* as the Elements that compose them, and thus, the Sameness of the Essences of the Intelligibles, passes through the Sameness of the Elemental Bodies, and manifests as the Sameness of the bodies in the Heavenly side of the Sensible Cosmos. It is for this reason that of these bodies all are immortal and incorruptible, these are not constructed, and in the true sense of the word are not composed. With these bodies of the Elemental Bodies in the Soul World, immortality ceases, and all below is more or less subject unto death.

15.   Whereas in all the rest of composed bodies, of each there is a certain number; for without number structure cannot be, or composition, or decomposition.

Now it is units that give birth to number and increase it, and being decomposed, are taken back again into themselves.

Matter is one; and this whole Cosmos—the mighty God and image of the mightier One, both with Him unified, and the conserver of the Will and Order of the Father—is filled full of Life.

Naught is there in it throughout the whole of Æon, the Father's [everlasting] Re-establishment, —nor of the whole, nor of its parts,—which doth not live.

For not a single thing that's dead, hath been, or is, or shall be in [this] Cosmos.

For that the Father willed it should have Life as long as it should be. Wherefore it needs must be a God.

Whereas in all the rest of composed bodies, of each there is a certain number; for without number structure cannot be, or composition, or decomposition.

All the other bodies aside from those that we have spoken of heretofore, are composed in accordance with number. These bodies are very different from the simple bodies that we have been examining, for these bodies are constructed according to number. It is in this way that bodies are composed, and likewise it is through the operation of number that all composed bodies are in their turn, decomposed,

This construction of composed bodies according to number is due to the fact that these other bodies are composed of the diverse elements. It is a mistake to assume that souls are simple entities, containing in them but one element. On the contrary, they are composed of a diversity of elements. It is in the Psyche that we find the first trace of the Four Natures, the Hot Nature, the Dry Nature, the Moist Nature and the Cold Nature. These are not in the Psyche strictly speaking Elements, they become this in the Pneuma or Spirit, but in Soul they are the four Natures. Now, Nature is the process of Genesis, that which brings things to birth, the process of being born. The four natures will, therefore, be the four-fold process of being born, the four-fold genesis. This process of genesis manifests through Heat, through Dryness, through Moisture and through Cold. It is in this way that the process of genesis differentiates the Psyche into Heat, Dryness, Moisture and Cold. This in reality means the genesis of the Hot Psyche, the Dry Psyche, the Moist Psyche and the Cold Psyche. These, therefore, become respectively the Soul of Heat, the Soul

of Dryness, the Soul of Moisture and the Soul of Cold.
Thus do we get the Four Psyches. Two of these are
related to the others as energies, while the other two
are related to them as bodies in a sense. The Moist Nature and the Cold Nature are passive and hence passible,
while the Hot Nature and the Dry Nature are Active
and hence we might call them passionate in their action.
In their combinations, the Hot Nature energizes the Cold
Nature which is to it as a Matrix, and the Dry Nature
energizes the Moist Nature which is to it as a matrix.
It is through the conjunction of the Hot Nature with the
Cold Nature, and the conjunction of the Dry Nature with
the Moist Nature that the bodies are composed, which on
this plane, are of course souls, on the Spiritual Plane
they will be spirits, and on the Physical Plane they will
of course be physical bodies. This action of the Four
Natures has the effect of differentiating the Psyche into
what might be termed Atoms so long as we understand
that it is Atoms of Psyche of which we are speaking.
What we mean is the Units of Psyche, in the sense of
Psyche being here Stuff or Matter, and these Units of
Psyche, the Units of that Psychic Stuff or Psychic Matter. We will use the term Unit to express this Atom if
you like of Psyche. Remember there are four kinds of
these Units, the Unit of Psychic Heat, the Unit of Psychic Dryness, the Unit of Psychic Moisture and the Unit
of Psychic Cold. The Units of Heat and of Dryness are
Positive, while the Units of Moisture and the Units of
Cold are Negative. Structure of bodies is by reason of
the combination in accordance with number, of these
units. Thus it is that all bodies are composed through
the numerical combination of the units, and hence, decomposition of bodies results from the separation of
these units the one from the other.

Now it is units that give birth to number and increase it, and, being decomposed, are taken back again into themselves.

Number grows out of the union of these psychic units. It is the proportion in which the four kinds of units are united that determines the *nature* of the body. We use the term *nature* advisedly, for the units are of one or the other of the four natures, and in proportion as they are united, so will the *nature* of the body be, seeing that these units will, in proportion to their relative number, determine the genesis within the body thus constructed. Number is merely the result and likewise the means of the proportional combination of the four kinds of units, it is through the combination of the units according to numerical proportion that bodies are composed. This being the case, it will of course follow that decomposition of bodies, through the disintegration of their numerical arrangement, will separate the units, and restore them to their original free condition, as they were before they entered into the composition of the bodies. This being the case, construction, composition and decomposition all depend upon the association of the units in their numerical combination. The units then are in the nature of bodies that are assembled together, and number is the action of energy upon them. In this way are souls composed and decomposed through construction and decomposition. What is here stated with reference to souls is true of all other bodies as well. From this, you will see at a glance the true method of Transmutation. The transmutation of a body is merely a question of changing its Number, by which we mean the numerical proportion of the units of the Four Natures and in this way changing the nature of the body. This is the only secret in the Science of Metamorphosis also. All the diversity in the bodies in the universe is merely due to the diversity in the numerical arrangement of the units of the Four Natures. But the mistake that has been made by the Alchemists has been in assuming that they could consummate the transformation in physical bodies without acting upon the psychic and spiritual bodies as well. When they have learned that the Great Work must be accomplished on all Three Planes simultaneously, and have grasped this secret of the four natures, their units and the factor of number in their association and their combination as the key to the composition of all bodies, there will be no difficulty in the work of Practical Alchemy. This is also the Key to Magic and to all the Miraculous Powers of the Prophets and Saviours of the world. These that we have indicated are the only factors involved.

Matter is one; and this whole Cosmos—the mighty God and image of the mightier One, both with Him unified, and the conserver of the Will and Order of the Father—is filled full of Life.

The first lesson to learn here is that Matter is one, that is to say, we are not dealing with a multiplicity of material elements, but with one, indivisible Matter, out of which all the elements appear. We are of course, not pretending that there are not a great many different material elements, but we do contend that these are all so many differentiations of the one Matter. Matter as used here, primarily refers to Physical Matter, but this in its purest form. The Cosmos is called the mighty God, because it is the manifestation of all the activity of the Supreme Divinity. It is, therefore, called the image of God, being His Image in the same sense that Mind is the image of God, though of course the Cosmos is an image of God on a much lower scale than is the Mind. The Cosmos is the Order manifested by God in the world of Matter, but using Matter here in the sense of the Substratum of Nature. Cosmos is the Image of God, and is likewise unified with God. That is to say, God

and Cosmos are in fact *one*, seeing that all of the activity
of God is expressed in Cosmos, and Cosmos has nothing
in It save that which comes from God. Thus is Cosmos
one with God. Cosmos is also called the conserver of the
Will and Order of the Father, for the reason that the
Will and Order of the Father enter into Cosmos, and
remain there, none of either being lost, but all being conserved in Cosmos. The Will of the Father, the Supreme
Deity, is the Positive Force or Energy of God, the Centrifugal Energy generated within the Father and radi-
atèd forth from Him. It is the Power of God as Energy
and Force, and this in a Positive state. The statement
that Cosmos is the conserver of this Will of God means
that this Positive Will Force or Energy of God, enters
into Cosmos, and being retained there, it is conserved
in the sense that it is embodied, and utilized in the
Cosmic operations, so that no part of It is permitted to
lie idle, It is all expressed in the life and action of the
Cosmos. The same is true of the Order of the Father,
It is all expressed in and through the Order of the Cosmos. Thus, the Cosmos becomes the Receptacle in which
all the Will Force and the Order of the Father are received, and in which they are made manifest in the Cosmic operations and transfôrmations. It is in this way
that the Cosmos is filled full of Life, that is, becomes
literally a Pleroma or *fullness* of Life. Cosmos is then,
the Vessel or container of Life. Just as it is the Organ
of the Will of God, so is it the Pleroma of all Life. Let
us not misunderstand the meaning of Life as it is used
here. This Life is one of the Energies radiated from
God, the two principle ones of which are Light and Life.
Light is the pure energy which manifests as Mind, and
Life is that pure energy that manifests as Soul. In a
word, Life is the Energy that produces Soul as a result
of its contact with Substance. Thus is Cosmos indeed
the Second God, seeing that all of the Will and all of the
Order of the God Beyond All Name are received into

Cosmos, and that Cosmos is the Pleroma filled full of the Life of God, and that all of the Life of God remains in that Pleroma. It is indeed the continuation of the Ultimate God. Cosmos then is the continuation of the Essence of God through Manifestation, the first is God in essence, while the Second or Cosmos, is the same God in Action and in Manifestation.

Naught is there in it throughout the whole of Æon, the Father's [everlasting] Re-establishment, —nor of the whole, nor of its parts,—which doth not live.

The fundamental statement in this paragraph is, that there is nothing in Cosmos that does not live. This is stated both with reference to Cosmos as a whole, and likewise with reference to each and all of its several parts. If we look at the question logically we will see that this could not be any other way. Cosmos receives the totality of the Will Force of God, and is energized thereby. Likewise it receives into Its depths the totality of the Order of God and is ordered thereby. Also, Cosmos receives into Itself the totality of the Life of God, and is vitalized thereby. As all the Energy that enters in Cosmos is the Will Force of God, it follows that Cosmos is energized by nothing but the Energy of God, hence it is energized by the Energy of Immortality, which will, of course, mean that there is nothing to energize it other than as immortal. The Order established in Cosmos through the action of the Order of God, will of course be an Immortal Order, and hence there will be nothing in Cosmos to order anything but the living and the immortal. And as the Life of God fills the Cosmos, it will follow that there can be no part of Cosmos not acted upon by that Life, and hence every particle of Cosmos will be vitalized by the Life of God, thus will Cosmos become the Pleroma of Immortality. Being

filled in all of its parts with Life, there will be in no part
of Cosmos room for death. Æon is the everlasting
Re-establishment of the Father. This means that Æon
or Eternity is the perpetual re-establishment of that
which God has established. This of course means that
Æon repeats to infinity, whatever God does. As this
Æon is in perpetual contact with Cosmos, it follows
that Æon is everlastingly re-establishing in Cosmos,
whatever *is* in God. This will mean that there can never
be any thing in God that is not at the same time established by Æon in Cosmos. Likewise there can never
be any thing in Cosmos that is not also in God. Thus,
through Æon, Cosmos is the perfect Image of God, an
image in which the totality and the perfection of God
are reproduced at all times. Thus is Cosmos the perfect and the everlasting Reflection and Manifestation of
God. Hence, there can be no part of it, which is not
alive, every part of this Cosmos must Live. By this
we mean that Life is the *Essential Nature* of every part
of the Cosmos and there is, and can be, absolutely no
exception to this rule.

For not a single thing that's dead, hath been, or is,
or shall be in [this] Cosmos.

This merely means that there is nothing dead in the
Cosmos, nothing there dies, neither has there anything
ever died there, nor will there ever die anything that is
there now or ever will be there. Death in the Cosmos
there never has been, there is not at this time, and there
never will be in time to come. This could otherwise not
be, seeing that every particle of Cosmos is filled full of
Life, there is then no room for death in that which is
filled full of life, it can only live, it can never die. Whatever comes to be in the Cosmos never ceases to be. It
will at once appear that this could not be otherwise, if
we bear in mind that every thing that is in Cosmos is
merely the re-establishment there of something that has

come from God. Every thing in Cosmos being nothing
else than the Æonian reproduction of an act of God,
this reproduced act can no more be dissolved in the
Cosmos, than can one of the acts of God be destroyed.
As all the movements of Cosmos are movements of the
Life of God, Cosmos in every one of Its movements and
states must be as Immortal as is God. Therefore,
nothing in it ever dies, has ever died, or will ever die in
the future. Whatever once comes into existence in
Cosmos, must live there without end.

For that the Father willed it should have Life as
long as it should be. Wherefore it needs must be a
God.

The statement that the Father willed anything, means
that the action of the Will Force of the Father literally
brought that condition into being. For Him to will
anything, simply means that through the action of His
Will Force, that thing is created. To say that the Father
willed that the Cosmos should have Life as long as it
should be, means one and only one thing, viz., the action
of the Will Force of the Father gave Life to Cosmos,
and established Life as the Essentiality of Cosmos, in
such a way that Cosmos could not exist save as the
Pleroma of Life. As the Will Force of the Father in-
fuses Life into the Cosmos as long as the Cosmos shall
continue to be, there can then, never be a time when
the Cosmos or any part of it shall be without Life, hence
there can never be a time when death shall be experienced by the Cosmos or any part of it, seeing that in
which is filled full of Life, there can be no room for
death. As the Cosmos is merely the re-establishment of
the Life of God, there can never be a time when Cosmos
will cease to be, so long as God lives, seeing that God
lives in His actions, and these actions of God are Eter-
nally re-established as the Cosmos, and as all this is an
act of God's Life through His Will of course the Cosmos

is as enduring as is God. As the Cosmos is this re-establishment of God and of His Life, its Essence being Life, then it must be a God, seeing that nothing else but a God could have Life as its essentiality.

16. How, then, O son, could there be in the God, the image of the Father, in the plentitude of Life—dead things?

For that death is corruption, and corruption is destruction.

How then could any part of that which knoweth no corruption be corrupted, or any whit of him the God destroyed?

Tat. Do they not, then, my father, die—the lives in it, that are its parts?

Her. Hush, son!—led into error by the term in use for what takes place.

They do not die, my son, but are dissolved as compound bodies.

Now dissolution is not death, but dissolution of a compound; it is dissolved not so that it may be destroyed, but that it may become renewed.

For what is the activity of life? Is it not motion? What then in Cosmos is there that hath no motion? Naught is there, son!

How, then, O son, could there be in the God, the image of the Father, in the plentitude of Life—dead things?

Cosmos is described under three heads, as a God, as the image of the Father, and as the plentitude of Life. Now, the question is, how can dead things exist in either one of these, to say nothing of all three of them? Cosmos is a God for the reasons that we have indicated and as the very essence of godhood is the giving of life, how can there be any dead things in God? We have also

shown how it is that the Cosmos is the image of the
Father, and if Cosmos be the image of the Father, there
can be nothing in Cosmos which is not likewise in the
Father, and which has not been imaged in Cosmos by
the Father, how then can any dead thing be in the
Father? and if there be no dead thing in the Father,
there is nothing in the Father to image a dead thing in
Cosmos. Nothing in the Father can be imaged by a dead
thing, and as there is nothing in Cosmos that is not imaged by the Father, how then can there be dead things
in the image of the Father? This being true, how can
dead things be in Cosmos? Cosmos is also the plentitude of Life, and in the plentitude of Life, how can there
be any dead things? Thus we see that there can be
nothing dead in the Cosmos.

For that death is corruption, and corruption is destruction.

Death is nothing other than the corruption of the elements that go to make up a thing. Corruption leads to
destruction, and this, destruction in the sense of the extinction of the elements that go to make up the thing, together with the dissolution of the *nature* of that thing.
It is not destruction so long as the elements of which
the body is composed remain, the elements themselves
must be extinguished before there can be any such condition as destruction. It is in this way that corruption
leads to destruction, through the corruption of the elements of which the things are composed, and hence that
these elements shall cease to exist even as elements. It
is in this sense that we must view death in order to see
that there can of necessity be no such thing.

How then could any part of that which knoweth no
corruption be corrupted, or any whit of him the God
destroyed?

Hermes takes the position that Cosmos knows no corruption, seeing that Cosmos is but the image of God, and is energized by nothing else than the Energies of God. This being the case, there is in Cosmos, both in whole and in each of its parts, nothing to corrupt, and nothing to cause corruption, therefore, how can it know corruption? And if it knows no corruption, if corruption is foreign to the essentiality of Cosmos itself, how is it possible for any part of Cosmos to be corrupted? He holds that Cosmos is a God, being the image of the Ultimate God, now the question is, how can any whit of a God be destroyed? As every part and activity of Cosmos is nothing else than an activity of the Ultimate God, how can this Divine Action be interrupted? All the energies of Cosmos being the reflected Energies of God, how can they ever cease to energize, and therefore, how can that which their energizing keeps alive, ever cease to live as a result of their energizing, and hence how can it ever be destroyed? Cosmos being both in whole and in part, merely a continuation of the life and activity of God, and thus its perpetuation being a condition essential to the continuation of God Himself, how can any part of Cosmos be destroyed? Of course we see from this, that Cosmos can no more be subject unto destruction than God Himself can be subject unto destruction. The Cosmos being the Image of God and at the same time God in Action, of course it is as permanent as is God, hence there can be in Cosmos no destruction. For no energy of God can ever cease to energize, hence no part of Cosmos can ever cease to be, hence there is in Cosmos no destruction.

Tat. Do they not, then, my father, die—the lives in it, that are its parts?

While Tat is able to understand that the Cosmos as a whole knows no death, but ever remains as it is, yet he

assumes that the lives in the Cosmos must die, and that
the Cosmos is perpetuated through a continual change
in those lives, by reason of the death of one generation
of the lives, and the genesis of another generation of
the lives. Of course this shows that he has not understood the true nature of the Cosmos, which is, the Order
of the activities of the Energy of God, the Field of Its
operations and the sum-total of all things born. This
being the case, all the lives in Cosmos are in reality
born out of the energizing of Cosmos by the Life of God,
hence their energies being deathless, it must follow as a
matter of course, that these lives are likewise deathless.
Likewise, Tat fails to realize that Cosmos is the sum-
total of all things born, and that any whole is equal to
the sum of its parts, hence, were the lives that are the
parts of Cosmos to die, it could not be that Cosmos, the
total of all things born, could be deathless, if the things
that went to make up Cosmos were to die. In other
words, things which singly are subject to death, cannot
be deathless en masse. Tat evidently undertakes to separate the Cosmos from the lives in it, to separate the
Cosmos as a whole from all of its several parts. This
is an old error that many have fallen into, it is the error
of believing in *Things in Themselves*, Tat believes in a
Cosmos *in itself*, which is distinct from the things that
go to make it up. If the Cosmos is the sum-total of all
things born, then it has a dual aspect, it is first the process of bearing all things, and second the things born as
a result of that process. Now, it is astonishing how
many people really believe that there can be a process
of bearing, independent of the things that are born
thereby. Of course this is out of the question, there is
a process of bearing, simply because there is a continual
sequence of things coming into being; but were there no
particular things being born, there would be no process
of bearing things possible, just as a mother is one because she bears children, motherhood depending upon

the child being engendered. Should the things born, cease to be born, there would in that event be no process of bearing things. Likewise, the character and the nature of the process of bearing, must be identical with the character and the nature of the things born. This being true, it will follow that if the Cosmos as a whole is free from death, the lives in it, which are parts of it, and which collectively constitute it, must likewise be free from death.

Her. Hush, son!—led into error by the term in use for what takes place.

The difficulty is that we speak from appearances rather than from reality, and so we speak of death, when we in reality mean the passing of a thing from our view, and not its destruction. This confusion is due to our mistaking the sensible for the real, and thus when a thing ceases to present itself to the senses we are prone to think that it has ceased to be. The term in use being death, and it is used for that disappearance from the world of visibility, which to those who depend upon their senses, means a cessation of existence, death comes to mean merely the disappearance of a thing from the state of visibility. But death is in reality the total destruction of the thing in its elements, and this confusion is merely due to the fact that the ignorant do not know that when a thing ceases to be visible, it still continues to be invisible, hence, to them, cessation of visibility is the same as destruction. It is for this reason that they call this disintegration of a body, death, or destruction. One must not be deceived by the terms in use, but must seek to understand their true inwardness. In this connection we must not be deceived by the fallacy that words are made proper by usage, this is absolutely untrue. Words are the expression of certain definite ideas, and because the un-men in their ignorance confuse these ideas with certain phenomena in their experience, that is no reason why we should use the word to express their delusions in lieu of the reality which the word in itself stands for. We must learn to trace back words to their origins in our thinking, if we do not feel free to do so in our usage of them. The trouble is, words are the vehicles for the expression of ideas, but at the same time they tend to become fetters for the binding and limitation of our ideas as well. If we accept of a word as being the symbol of a certain idea, we will use it to express that idea, hence there is danger of having our ideas warped by the words we use. We may use the words in common usage, so long as we do not use them as equivalent to the sense in which they are understood by the multitude. In other words, should you use words in the sense in which they are defined in Webster's Dictionary, you will ultimately find yourself thinking in the mold furnished you in Webster's Dictionary, so that you will be no wiser than was Webster, and will think as he did. Rather must you ascertain the Origins of Words and their inner meaning, and whenever you have occasion to use them, use them from the standpoint of your own philosophy, not from the standpoint of there meaning as it is associated with them in the consciousness of the mindless un-men. In this way, words will not bind your thought, you will not think in subjection to words, but will use them to express your ideas, and you will not be limited to the plane of thought of the un-men. It will make little difference whether the un-men understand what you are talking about or not, this is of little moment compared with the danger of taking on their complexion of thought, and thinking as they do, which may happen if you speak the language of Webster rather than the language of the Logos as it is manifested in your own ideas.

They do not die, my son, but are dissolved as compound bodies.

The lives in Cosmos, that is the parts of Cosmos do not die, they are simply dissolved as compound bodies. This being true, it follows that these lives in Cosmos have compound bodies, otherwise they could not be dissolved as compound bodies. We must be very careful in our examination of these lives in Cosmos, otherwise we will be confused as to their nature. It must be borne in mind that the lives in Cosmos are both within and out of, Cosmos. There are the Germs or Monads of those lives, which ever subsist in Cosmos, but the lives in the proper sense of the word are born out of Cosmos, and are in turn drawn into Cosmos to be born out of it again. Of course in this sense we are speaking of Cosmos as the Intelligible Cosmos. When the lives are born out of Cosmos it means that they are born into Psyche, and hence these lives are in reality souls, it is as souls that they exist as individualized lives. But the lives also are compound bodies, that is to say, they manifest as compound bodies, and all compound bodies are compounded from the Four Elements of Earth, Air, Fire and Water. Thus, these compound bodies are Spirit, and also as a general thing, these bodies are compounded from Matter, that is to say, Physical Matter. The Spirit Bodies are composed, but not compounded, it is the physical bodies that are strictly compounded. Now, what passes for death, in the case of these lives in Cosmos, is merely the dissolution of their compound bodies into the elements that have gone to constitute them. It is this dissolution of the compound bodies into the diverse elements that passes for death, but the body still lives in the elements that were united in order to form the compound, previously the elements were joined to form the compound, now they have separated the one from the other, but there is just as much matter after the dissolution of the compound as there was while the compound continued. Likewise, this matter is of precisely the same elements, in exactly the same proportion that they were present in the compound. This being the case, there has been no destruction and hence no death, there has merely been the cessation of the compound which is the body.

Now dissolution is not death, but dissolution of a compound; it is dissolved not so that it may be destroyed, but that it may become renewed.

In dissolution there is no death, for the reason that there is not the extinction of any element. There is merely the dissolution of a compound, but all that went into the compound still remains, it is merely freed from the compound state, but is not destroyed. A Compound is dissolved not as a means unto its destruction, but rather as a means unto its renewal. In this way, every compound that ever has been will be again. Compounds are dissolved, and their elements drawn up into Cosmos to be again brought forth as new compounds, and yet they are identically the same compounds that they were before their dissolution. What we have here is a series of reincarnations as compounds, each one terminated by a process of dissolution in order that all may be drawn into Cosmos and be re-born in the fullness of time. This being the case, there is no such thing as death, but rather a sequence of alterations from the compounded to the dissolved state of bodies and back again. This is the periodicity of life and has no element of death in it. It is rather that the lives live in two states of life, the compounded and the un-compounded or dissolved states of life. It is the sequence of birth, dissolution of the compound, and renewal of the compound state through re-birth that we have; but there is in all this no element of death, hence, none of the lives or any of the things in Cosmos die, therefore, all in Cosmos is as deathless as is Cosmos itself, that is to say, as deathless as God.

For what is the activity of life? Is it not motion?

What then in Cosmos is there that hath no motion?
Naught is there, son!

The activity of life is motion. This means that motion
is the activity that constitutes life. Life in other words
is simply the sequence of actions going on to infinity, and
all action is motion. This being the case, death would
mean that motion had ceased, hence there was no action,
and if no action, then there would be no life; for life and
motion are one. There can be no dead thing, until there
is a time when there is a body that does not move, that
is deprived of all motion. This is out of the question.
It would be contrary to all the principles involved in the
nature of a body, were it to be destitute of motion. In
fact it would not be a body at all. The very essentiality
of a body is its passibility. And the essentiality of
passibility is in its responsiveness to movement. In
other words, a body is a body for one and only one reason; because it is possible, were it not passible it would
not be a body. A body is passible for one and only one
reason, because it is subject unto motion, which places
it in the category of the *Moved,* and it is to be classed as
the *moved* because energy or passion distinct from itself,
moves it; but it moves it because it acts upon the passible body from within, never without. Hence, a body
is a body only because it is permeated by energy which
acting upon the body as passion, moves the body, without such motion it would not be a body. This being the
case, as there is no body that is not moved, seeing that its
Esse as a body is in the fact that it is moved; and as there
is not motion, apart from the act of moving on the part
of the *Mover;* and as the activity of motion is life, there
can be no body that is not alive, hence a dead body is
something that even the power of God cannot produce,
hence there are no dead bodies, but only living bodies.
Then, there is nothing in the whole Cosmos that has no
motion, therefore, in all the Cosmos there is nothing

dead, but all things in the Cosmos are alive. For this
reason, we are able to see that there is no death, but perpetual change. It is a process of ever-transforming life,
that manifests through a series of compound bodies, a
series reaching from infinity to infinity. A series reaching from and out of, "Beginnings boundless unto and
into an endless end." This is the true secret of the immortality of all things, of the eternity of matter. It is
not the puerile theory of an Ego which as a form or
entity passes from one compound body into another, but
rather the continual evolution of energy and force, likewise substance, through an infinity of transformations,
a process that always has been going on, and always will
go on so long as Eternity shall endure. This is the
true Alchemy, the compounding of bodies from the finer
substances and energies, and when these compounds have
reached maturity and perfection, they are dissolved into
substances and energies once again. The process of
compounding bodies is the descending from the Subtle
into the Gross, the materialization of the subtle essences.
The process of dissolution is the process of ascending
from the Gross into the Subtle, the transmutation of the
compound bodies into the finer essences. It is in this
way that the entire material universe is transformed and
transmuted from one state into another, and thus,
through the interplay of compounding and dissolution,
of compound bodies and free energies, is rendered possible the Eternal Progress and continual advancement of
the Matter of which the Universe is composed. There is
seen to be no fine gradation between God and Nature,
between Cosmos and Matter, between Heaven and Earth,
but rather is there the one Principle assuming diverse
forms and states but through all of its myriad changes,
remaining ever the same. What men in their ignorance
call death is then the gateway of life, the preparation for
the next birth. It is simply another case of Genesis and

Change. Thus composition and decomposition are the
two poles of Life, if we may use the term, but in all this
Cosmos there is no death for all is life, and the diverse
compounds of Cosmic Life.

LESSON VIII.

CHANGE AND SENSATION.

17. *Tat.* Doth not Earth even, father, seem to thee to have no motion?

Her. Nay, son; but rather that she is the only thing which, though in very rapid motion, is also stable.

For how would it not be a thing to laugh at, that the Nurse of all should have no motion, when she engenders and brings forth all things?

For 'tis impossible that without motion one who doth engender, should do so.

That thou shouldst ask if the fourth part is not inert, is most ridiculous; for that the body which doth have no motion, gives sign of nothing but inertia.

Tat. Doth not Earth even, father, seem to thee to have no motion?

The teaching that has been given indicates that there is no such thing as an inert body. This is of course the obvious truth; for it has been clearly shown that it is passibility and hence mobility that constitutes a mass of matter a body, the Esse of body being its passibility under the action of motion, hence there could not possibly be a body that is devoid of motion. It would then appear that there is in all the universe no body that is devoid of motion. Tat is confused by this, for he thinks that the Earth is a body that has no motion. This ques-

(146)

tion about the motion of the Earth must be understood
in three separate and distinct senses; it means the physical earth, the organic physical matter of the entire
Universe, including all of the heavenly bodies, and likewise it refers to the Element Earth. Applied to the
physical earth, the question may be viewed under two
separate heads: there is the question as to the passibility
or impassibility of the particles composing the earth,
is it a dense body, moving only en masse, or do the molecules of the earth separately move? and also does the
earth as a body move, or is it stationary in the midst of
the Sensible Cosmos? The Text would seem to indicate
that Tat shared in the belief that the earth was a stationary body in the midst of the Sensible Cosmos, and
that all the heavenly bodies moved around the earth as
their Center. This we know was the belief of the un-
initiated at that time, and it would not be surprising if
Tat was one who shared in the common opinion of the
time. If such was his opinion, the answer of Hermes,
indicates that the Hermetic Teaching was quite other
than this view. It would show that he understood the
motions of the earth, and other parts of the writing of
Hermes go to show that he did teach the rotation of the
earth. If the question of Tat had reference to the question of whether the earth moved en masse, or if the body
of the earth was endowed with the property of molecular vibration, then the answer of Hermes would indicate that he certainly taught that the earth was a
vibrating mass of molecules. If the question related to
the physical Universe, then the answer would show that
both molecular vibration, and motion en masse was characteristic of all the heavenly bodies. If the question was
asked in reference to the Element of Earth, then the
answer would indicate that Hermes taught that this
Element is not inert, but on the contrary, in constant
motion in all of its molecules and atoms. At least one
thing is clear, Hermes was repudiating the doctrine of

the inertia of Earth in all of its details. There is enough
here to indicate that the idea of the modern Scientists
that the Ancients knew nothing of the motion of the
earth, is absolutely erroneous when applied to the Ini-
tiates of the Esoteric Philosophy. The trouble is that
they have judged the Ancient Philosophers by what they
taught the general public, and not by their Esoteric
Teachings. Of course it is difficult for them to understand how these Philosophers should wish to conceal
their knowledge in regard to profane science from the
multitude. Our answer is that there was no such thing
in that time as profane science, the Earth being Divine
in their Theology, it followed that whatever was known
about the earth was Sacred Knowledge. In other words,
both Geology and Physics were departments in Theology
not in Physical Science as now, and hence, to disclose
their knowledge with reference to the Earth would be to
make public some of the most Sacred Tenets of their
Esoteric Theology. This will explain why they were so
very secret about these things, and it will also show us
why, in order to understand the Physics, Chemistry,
Astronomy, and Geology of the Ancient Philosophers
we must study their Theology, for it is only there that
we find what they really knew about such things. Now,
it must be borne in mind that it is in just such Sermons
as the present one, that we find the very purest form of
the Ancient Theology, and hence, here we will get at the
very deepest secrets of the Ancient Science. It was to
get at this kind of truth that Tat asked this question,
and for that reason the answer of Hermes is of such
transcendent importance.

Her. Nay, son; but rather that she is the only
thing which, though in very rapid motion, is also
stable.

The contention of Hermes is that the Earth is in very
rapid motion, but that with this great rapidity of motion,

the stability of the Earth is yet maintained. If we apply this to the motion of the earth as a body, we will find the meaning to be this: the Earth moves very rapidly along the path of her orbit, yet she never deviates from her fixed course, revolving around her Center of Gravity in such a manner as to preserve her path, and thus is she stable, and not variable in her course. If Earth is here used with reference to the entire Physical Universe, the meaning will be, while each one of the heavenly bodies is in very rapid motion, yet, it is so arranged that their relative positions are never shifted, and thus the stability of the Universe is at all times preserved. If he refers to the molecular motion of the Earth, he means that while the molecules are in constant motion, and while they are all the time changing their relative positions, yet, the stability of the Earth as a body is never effected. If he refers to the Element of Earth, he means that the motions within this Element never cause it to be any thing else than Earth. In any event, he is speaking of a stability that is the result of the equalization of the diverse motions, rather than of a stable body, the stability of which is in contradistinction to motion.

For how would it not be a thing to laugh at, that the Nurse of all should have no motion, when she engenders and brings forth all things?

The Earth is here represented as the engenderer, the bearer and the Nurse of all things. It should be understood that to the Hermetic Philosophers as well as to the Platonists the Earth was an Animal. This has confused many owing to fact that they thought it was a mere figure of speech, being unable to realize that it was a literal statement of fact. The Earth is an Animal that sexually engenders as a result of conception, that gives birth in the sexual sense, and then that suckles that which she has brought forth. We still hear the expression, Mother

Earth, but few there are who understand how literally true is the expression. The Earth is literally the Mother of all things of the Earth. She becomes pregnant, and as a result of her pregnancy, engenders all things as Foetii in her Womb. When they are come to maturity, she through a process of parturition bears them as a Mother bearing babies. After their birth, all things are nursed by the Earth as Wet Nurse, just as the Mother or Wet Nurse suckles the Child, only in the case of the Earth Mother, her children are never weaned, but are nursed at the breasts of the Mother so long as they live. All of the Four Elements are present in the Earth. She has the Fire in her center, and the Air and Water are present in the Body of Earth. Not only are the Four Elements present in her composition, but all of the Eighty-six Chemical Elements are likewise present in her composition. It is through the chemical affinity of these Elements that her life and action are largely brought about. All of her molecules are in constant motion, and through their motion, diverse Zones of activity are formed. These Zones perform the same function in her life that the various Plexii and Ganglions in any other body perform. Likewise there are Billions and Billions of Cells in the body of the Earth, performing precisely the same functions as do the Living Cells in a human body. Again, in the body of the earth will be found the innumerable minute lives, that are the basis of all her life and consciousness. Not only is the earth physical, but she also has her own Life Force, her own Spirit and her Own Soul. The Earth is the self-fecundating Mother, who is perpetually fecundating herself. As a result of this process, countless billions of foetii are conceived and gestated in her innumerable wombs and made ready for birth. These lives must first be conceived in the Soul of the Earth, then in the Spirit of the Earth, they must be vitalized with the Breath of Life of the Earth, and then they are conceived and gestated within the body of the

Earth. They are born when they spring into existence on the surface of the Earth. The theory that all things come from a Germ in the Earth is in perfect harmony with this view of the Biology of Mother Earth, though it falls far short of the rich reality that we are speaking of here. When New Germs are introduced into the Earth, it means that the Earth is the Female into whose fruitful Womb has been dropped the Seed from Higher Realms. This is particularly the work of the Genii, for in this way are all Genii initiated. It is not only through the spontaneous fruitfulness of the Earth Mother that all new plants are brought forth, but it is her engendering and bearing that causes all plants to spring up year after year. When men plant seed in the Earth, they are merely doing what the plant would do of itself were it let alone. It is the Earth Mother that is impregnated and conceives as a result of her fecundation by these seed, and in time bears the plant again. When the plant grows it is being nursed through its roots which are in the ground, it is sucking up the nourishment from the Breasts of the Earth Mother. Many forms of Animal Life are engendered within, and born forth from the Womb of Earth, and all Nursed by her, for all Animals live on the Vegetation which is born of the Earth Mother. Man is likewise the Nursling of the Earth Mother so long as he lives on the Physical Plane, and this is not all, when either Animal or Man passes from the Physical to the Spirit World as a rule he merely enters the Spirit of the Earth, and is nourished by her Spirit until the Soul leaves the Spirit and goes on to the Soul World, when his Soul is in the Soul of the Earth, and on his way to Reincarnation, the Soul of the Earth literally bears him into the Spirit of the Earth, which in turn, literally bears his Spirit into the Physical Plane when he enters the womb of his physical and human mother. Hence it is, that all earthly lives are engendered within the Womb of the Earth Mother, are gestated there and are born into outer life, and after this are Nursed by her so long as they live, and after their death the same process is gone through again to infinity. Of course there are Souls that are not confined to the Soul of the Earth, but they are in all cases Masters. It is this doctrine of the Motherhood of the Earth, that was so guarded in the ancient days, for it was a part of the Theology of their Religion. We need not go further into detail here, as this discussion belongs more to a treatise on Physical Alchemy than it does in a work of the character of the present treatise. We have shown how absolutely is the Earth the Engendering and Bearing as well as the Nursing Mother of all earthly things. Now the question raised by Hermes is this, how laughable would it be, for the Earth to be able to do all this, and yet have no motion! In view of what he has said previously in reference to the process of genesis it will be seen at once that genesis without motion is out of the question, and hence the Earth cannot be said to be without motion. All that is said here in reference to motion and the Physical Earth, will apply with equal force to all of the Physical Universe and to all of the Heavenly Bodies and also to the Element of Earth with their relation to motion. This being the case, the question of Tat is really something to laugh at.

For 'tis impossible that without motion one who doth engender, should do so.

The process of engendering bodies is a process of motion. This is due to the fact that all bodies are constructed from matter by reason of the action of force upon matter, by reason of which action, the matter is moved into position. All bodies are built up along Geometrical lines, the particles of matter being moved along definite lines in such a manner as to build up the body as a structure from the units of matter. All bodies will be found to be constructed in this way, and it is the way in which they are constructed that determines the character of life that may function in them. Such construction of bodies would not be possible unless there was motion within the bodies, to move the particles of matter of which the bodies are constructed. These particles or units of matter are the things moved, energy acting within the mass of matter is the mover, and the body is the space in which the motion takes place, and hence, there must be motion in all bodies, and likewise, bodies are the result of motion in the mass of matter from which the bodies were formed. Now, he has shown that all things were engendered in the Earth, and they were engendered as bodies, hence, they were all constructed from the matter of the Earth, hence there had to be motion in this matter in order to engender these bodies, therefore, there is of necessity motion in the Earth, not only this Earth, but the entire Sensible Cosmos and the Element of Earth as well. As genesis is through motion, it follows that it must be the motion of the Generatrix, hence the Generatrix possesses motion, and as she is the Earth, the Earth possesses motion.

That thou shouldst ask if the fourth part is not inert, is most ridiculous; for that the body which doth have no motion, gives sign of nothing but inertia.

By the fourth part, we are to understand the Fourth Element, Earth. It is most ridiculous to ask if this Element is inert, seeing that if it were inert and devoid of motion, then it would give sign of nothing but inertia, and this it does not do. We see material bodies move, and if they move, it is certain that they are moved by energy acting upon the molecules of matter composing their material bodies, hence there is motion in every such body. As all these bodies are produced by the Earth, it follows that she is able to produce from her self, bodies that move, and hence, bodies that are endowed with motion. Now, if the Earth were inert, she could not possibly produce that which moves, hence, the motion of these bodies must have been given to them by the Earth, and she would have to first possess the motion herself before she could give it to other bodies, hence the Earth is not inert, but is endowed with motion. This is true of all of the Element of Earth, for were this Element inert, it could not generate from its own substance bodies that move, hence the Element of Earth is not inert, but is endowed with motion. This of course does not mean that motion is initiated in this Element, but it does indicate the passibility of the Element to motion and shows that it is moved by the action of Energy upon it, and this action is within Earth, not outside of it.

18. Know, therefore, generally, my son, that all that is in Cosmos is being moved for decrease or for increase.

Now that which is kept moving, also lives; but there is no necessity that that which lives, should be all same.

For being simultaneous, the Cosmos, as a whole, is not subject to change, my son, but all its parts are subject unto it; yet naught [of it] is subject to corruption, or destroyed.

It is the terms employed that confuse men. For 'tis not genesis that constituteth life, but 'tis sensation; it is not change that constituteth death, but 'tis forgetfulness.

Since, then, these things are so, they are immortal all,—Matter [and] Life, [and] Spirit, Mind [and] Soul, of which whatever liveth, is composed.

Know, therefore, generally, my son, that all that is in Cosmos is being moved for decrease or for increase.

While there are of course exceptions to the rule, yet,

as a general rule, all things in the Cosmos are constantly being moved either for increase or for decrease. This means that all motions in the Cosmos as a general rule are for the purpose of causing increase or causing decrease. However, we must guard against the error of assuming design in the Cosmic motions, this is an error that is very seductive, but as a matter of fact there is no such thing as design in nature. It is not design but Causation that is the ruling principle in nature. By the statement that all motions in the Cosmos are for the purpose of causing increase or decrease, we should understand that all the motions in the Cosmos either cause increase or else cause decrease. There are then, two motions in the Cosmos, one of which has the effect of increasing every thing there, and the other has the effect of decreasing every thing in the Cosmos. This brings us back to the question of Genesis and Change or dissolution. All the motions in the Cosmos may be divided into two classes, one of which generates form, and the other disintegrates it. Thus, all the movements in the Cosmos are engaged in the work of creation, and in the dissolution of that which has been created. This is the sense in which all Cosmic movement is engaged in the work of Becoming through the alteration of Life and Death. This gives us the two modes of motion, one accumulative, and the other disintegrative. Thus all life is a process of generating forms, and of increasing them to the point of maturity of development, and then the gradual weakening of them, until they are dissolved. Thus, there is one form of Cosmic motion that nourishes all forms so that they grow, and in this way increase in size and strength, while the other form of Cosmic motion is one that draws the strength from all forms so that in the course of time they are sapped of their strength and die.

Now that which is kept moving, also lives; but

there is no necessity that that which lives, should be all same.

Motion and life are very nearly the same thing. Nothing can be kept moving without life. It is only the inert that can be dead, and as all things in Cosmos are kept moving, it follows that there is in Cosmos, nothing inert, hence there is nothing there that is dead, but all in it is alive. It is not necesary that we should undertake to show why it is that motion is life, that has been indicated in the earlier portion of this book, and we will have more light on the subject in the sequel. Suffice it to say that life is the result of motion. We are next brought into the Categories of *Same* and *Other*. There is no necessity that that which lives should be all *same*. This means that the mere fact of living does not render all the lives *same,* one life may be other than all other lives, and still be a life. The meaning of this is that particularity is quite consistent with this condition of life growing out of motion.

For being simultaneous, the Cosmos, as a whole, is not subject to change, my son, but all its parts are subject unto it; yet naught [of it] is subject to corruption, or destroyed.

The statement that the Cosmos is simultaneous means that throughout all of the Cosmos, motion is acting with equal force, there being no part of it where there is no motion, or any part of it where motion is more rapid than in any other part. Likewise, Cosmic motion does not start in one part of Cosmos and move from that part to some other part of Cosmos. Time and Space are not limitations upon the action of motion in Cosmos. On the other hand, every particle of Cosmos is simultaneously vibrant with live and energized by motion. This being true, the Cosmos as a whole is not subject to change, that is, there is not at one time one kind of a Cosmos, and at some other time, another kind of a Cosmos. In this way, Cosmos preserves its integrity as an unit, though it does go through diverse changes as to its separate parts. All of the different parts of Cosmos are changed and transformed, though the Cosmos as a whole is ever the same. This gives rise to the fact that Cosmos is ever changing, yet ever the same, that is Cosmos is ever changing in its separate parts, though ever the same as a whole. Yet, there is no part of the Cosmos that is subject to corruption, that is, no part of it is corrupted or disintegrated as to the Elements that go to compose it, hence no part of the Cosmos is ever destroyed. There is nothing that has ever been a part of Cosmos that ever ceases to be a part of Cosmos, and likewise there is no part of Cosmos that has not always been a part of Cosmos. The diverse parts of Cosmos go through innumerable changes, but they never cease to be. It is in this way that in the face of the innumerable changes through which all of the separate parts of Cosmos pass, yet Cosmos as a whole is for ever the same. In this way it is that all of the parts of Cosmos are immortal, seeing that the identity of no part of the Cosmos is ever lost. Nothing that has ever been will ever cease to be; though it may go through many places of existence during its mutations.

It is the terms employed that confuse men. For 'tis not genesis that constituteth life, but 'tis sensation; it is not change that constituteth death, but 'tis forgetfulness.

We must learn to think not in terms of words, but in terms of Ideas. Our thoughts must be clothed in ideas rather than in words. We must therefore, not be confused by the terms employed, but rather seek to get at the ideas which are expressed. It is not genesis that constitutes life. Genesis is in fact a process of life, and more than that it is an act of life. Of course we are speaking now of life as a principle or force. It is the activity of this life principle that generates form. As life is not dependent upon the genesis of form, it follows that it is in no sense dependent upon the form or forms generated. As genesis is an act of life, so is the form an expression and a vehicle of life. In the same way, change does not constitute death, for change is an act of life, hence all changes are wrought by life. As life brings about all changes, it follows that life itself is not effected by change and hence, life continues after the change. As life creates the body through genesis, and lives in the body that it has created, and likewise disintegrates the body through change, and lives on independent of the body, it follows that life itself is not effected by either genesis or change. Seeing that this is true respecting the principle of life in general, what constitutes a particular or individual life; life that starts at a given point in time, and is terminated at a given point in time, life in the sense of a single span of life? Life in this sense, depends upon sensation. We must not however confuse this sensation with the physical sensations, it is rather equivalent to the action of all of the Senses, and as that has been explained in the Philosophy of Alchemy we need not go into it at this time. We need only say that this sensation is the energizing of the being with the energies of all of the senses. It is this energizing by the senses and the thought, reasoning, psychic action, emotions and the physical actions that result from such energizing by the diverse senses that constitutes an individual span of life. Life in this sense is very closely identified with Consciousness. Life then, is a psychological proposition rather than something physical or material. This life will, therefore, continue so long as consciousness continues. Likewise, death is not identical with change, but on the other hand, death is identical with the cessation of sensation, and hence with the cessation of consciousness and of the psychic life of the individual. If one is able to carry with him all of his consciousness and his sensations from one incarnation into the next without losing any of it, he will in this way preserve a continuation of his sensations and consciousness and hence he will forget nothing, and therefore, he will experience no death. All things through their dissolution of form, lose for the time being their physical sensations, and hence their physical consciousness, and for this reason they die in the physical sense, seeing that there is a lapse of physical consciousness between two periods of physical life, but this breaking of the consciousness between the periods of two physical lives is all that there is of death. As this life that we are now talking about, is in no sense an essential life, but merely a reflex consciousness growing out of sensation, its death is likewise merely a phenomenon of reflex consciousness, and is in no sense an essential death. Life and death are then, merely phases of consciousness and memory, they have a subjective actuality, but absolutely no objective actuality. There are no dead things, there are only lapses of sensation and of consciousness. The distinction between life and death has no existence any where save in Psychology, it does not exist in nature, and should be eliminated from the vocabulary of Positive Science as it has no place there. We may speak of life and death as phases of individual consciousness, but to speak of them as conditions of actuality or reality, betrays the grossest ignorance of the Laws of Nature and Evolution.

Since, then, these things are so, they are immortal all,—Matter, [and] Life, [and] Spirit, Mind [and] Soul, of which whatever liveth, is composed.

Whatever lives is composed of Mind, Soul, Spirit, Life and Matter. Matter as used here refers to Physical Matter of course. Mind here is used in such a sense as

to include Reason as a part of Mind. All of these are
the Principles which go into the composition of all living
things. None of these Principles are subject to corruption or destruction in their elements. There is at all
times as much of either one of them as there has ever
been. None of their elements are ever decomposed as
elements, but are all of them used in the composition of
living things or else return into the great universal store-
house. This being true, all of these Principles are
immortal, seeing that they know no death. Likewise,
all of the material elements are immortal seeing that
they are not corrupted, though they are subject to change,
but change is not corruption or destruction. The changes
in sensation and consciousness do not effect the Principles of which all things are composed, and hence, the
Principles themselves know no death; for this reason
they are all immortal and immortality is their essence.

19. Whatever then doth live, oweth its immortality unto the Mind, and most of all doth man, he who
is both recipient of God, and co-essential with Him.

For with this life alone doth God consort; by
visions in the night, by tokens in the day, and by all
things doth He foretell the future unto him,—by
birds, by inward parts, by wind, by tree.

Wherefore doth man lay claim to know things past,
things present and to come.

Whatever then doth live, oweth its immortality
unto the Mind, and most of all doth man, he who is
both recipient of God, and co-essential with Him.

The immortality of all living things is due to the Mind,
this is true because it is the energy of the Mind that
moves all the other Principles and causes them to act
as they do. Soul is passible unto the action of the Mind,
but it is the Mind that moves all other things and hence,

Mind determines the course of life and action for all
the other principles. It is for this reason that all living
things are immortal because of the Mind, seeing that it
is the Mind that acts upon Soul, Spirit, Life and Matter
in such a way as to cause the diverse things to be brought
into being. While this is true of all living things, it is
true in an especial sense in the case of man. Man alone
is the recipient of God. As we have previously shown,
Mind acts upon the souls of the animals through their
nature, acting as an impersonal force, determining the
motions of their soul-stuff or Psyche. In man, however, Mind is individualized as the individual mind of
the man. Thus the activities of the Mind, act as Seed
of Thought which the Sense draws into the mind of man,
causing his mind to conceive thoughts after their image
and likeness. This being true, the human mind is able
to receive the Thoughts of the Divine Mind, making of
the mind of man the recipient of all the Thoughts of the
Divine Mind. In like manner are the Ideas of the Logos
received into the reason of man, and there become his
own ideas. In this way is God individualized in man. But
man is also co-essential with God, that is, God and man
have the same essence. We have previously seen how
it is that the Mind is the very essence of God. This
essence of God or Mind is present in man as his mind.
As the mind is of the same essence as the Mind, and as
this Mind is God's very essence, it follows that the mind
in man is of the essence of God, and hence through the
mind, man is co-essential with God. Man, through his
mind is, therefore, of the same essence as God, and also
he through his mind receives all of the Thoughts of
God so that he becomes the receptacle of God, and is in
this way recipient of God being of God's very essence.

For with this life alone doth God consort; by
visions in the night, by tokens in the day, and by all

things doth He foretell the future unto him,—by birds, by inward parts, by wind, by tree.

God consorts with man in the literal sense of being the consort of man. In this sense of his relationship to God, there are no men, they are all women. We mean literally that all men are the wives of God, and that He is the husband of all humanity. The mind of man is the womb which receives all of the Seed of Thought from the Mind, which is the essence of God, and which contains the Spermal Seed of God. In this way, these Spermal Seed of God act as the Seed of Thought which entering the matrix of the mind in man, impregnate it, causing this mental matrix to become fecundated with these Seed, and to sexually conceive thought. It is in this way that all thought in the mind is conceived and thus borne into action. Bear in mind that we are speaking now of the mind and of its thinking, not of the psychological reactions of the soul to the energizing by the senses. All of this mental life of man is the result of the impregnation and consequent fecundation of his mind by the Seed of Thought from God. This is literally a case of mental congress between the Mind and the mind in man. It is in this sense that God is the consort of man and man the consort of God. This is what is meant by God consorting with man, it means the literal sexual *marriage* between God and man, the *nuptial union* of God and man. Man is the only life with which God consorts in this way. In the mystical sense, therefore, all men are women, they are the women of God. To the wise, this will explain many things. He next goes on to explain the nature of the conceptions resulting from this consorting of God with Man. One form of this conception is visions in the night. This of course refers to those visions that are undoubtedly of Divine origin. They are due to the action of the energies of God on the mind of man, causing the manifestation to take the form of *sense* rather than the form of *thought*. All this takes place during the night, while the outer senses of man are dormant, permitting the senses of the Mind to have full play in connection with the mind of the man and its senses. During the day, when the outer senses are active, there are still tokens that show to his consciousness that the Seed from God are impregnating his mind. These are not the only ways by which man is able to know the future, for there are many ways that the Mind acts upon the mind in man, thereby enabling one to know the future. Seeing that God knows all about the future, and when the God Thought impregnates the mind of man, and there conceives a similar thought, man will have the same knowledge that was expressed in that particular God Thought. In this way is man able to know the future seeing that this knowledge has entered into him as his mind is recipient of all the Sense-and-Thought of God. Then we are informed that this knowledge is also communicated through Augury, by flying birds, by the inward parts of animals, by the wind and by trees. The sense in which such divination is true is that one must interpret the portents, and his interpretation is from within, not from without, that is, he attributes to the portents, that consciousness of the future which his mind has conceived as a result of its fecundation by the Seed of God. There is not, and never has been any such thing as Scientific Augury, it is merely a means of calling into the psychic consciousness that which is present in the mental consciousness, and that is born in the mind as a result of her having been impregnated by the Seed of Thought from God, and thereby conceiving the thoughts that give birth to the consciousness.

Wherefore doth man lay claim to know things past, things present and to come.

In the mind consciousness there is neither limitation of time or space. The Mind is that which determines all the operations within all of the lower Principles, and hence all the operations of Causation are the effects of the action of the Mind. The mind of man being impregnated by the energies of the Mind, is thereby, made conscious of that that is transpiring in the universe. In this way, does man know all that is going on at the present, all that has transpired in the past, seeing that it is preserved in the memory of the Common Mind, and all that is to transpire in the future, seeing that he has within him, the seeds that are to bring forth all that there is to be at any future time. This consorting of the Mind with the mind of man, renders the latter conscious of the sources of all future things. As all things are produced by Fate, as Fate is the effect of the Mind, and as the Mind is reproduced in the mind of a man, it follows of necessity that the man shall know what is to be brought about by Fate, thence he will know the future as well as the present and the past, seeing that he is able to know all that is in the Mind of God. All this is because he is the consort of God, because God is the consort of the mind of man. Man is the Spouse of God, and the mind of man is the womb perpetually fecundated by her Divine Spouse. Of course, this is not to be understood as being true of the un-man, but only of one who has come to the realization of all of his powers as a man.

LESSON IX.

The Conception and Contemplation of God.

20.   Observe this, too, my son; that each one of the
other lives inhabiteth one portion of the Cosmos,—
aquatic creatures water, terrene earth, and aery
creatures air; while man doth use all these,—earth,
water, air, [and] fire; he seeth heaven, too, and doth
contact it with [his] sense.

But God surroundeth all, and permeateth all, for
He is energy and power; and it is nothing difficult,
my son, to *conceive* God.

Observe this, too, my son; that each one of the
other lives inhabiteth one portion of the Cosmos,—
aquatic creatures water, terrene earth, and aery
creatures air; while man doth use all these,—earth,
water, air, [and] fire; he seeth heaven, too, and doth
contact it with [his] sense.

Besides the distinctions that we have already noticed,
there are other distinctions between man and the other
creatures. We have seen the psychological distinctions
between man and the other lives, we have also noticed
his relation to God, a relation and intercourse that is
not participated in by any other life, we must now see
the other powers that man has in excess of the animal
lives. This distinction is to be observed in the fact that
all other physical lives are confined to one portion of
the Cosmos, being limited to one of the elements. Aquatic creatures are confined to the water. They have no
power of locomotion any where except in the water, and

(165)

they also breathe the air that is contained in the water. They are provided with an apparatus for breathing that is perfectly adapted to extracting the air from the water, but which is incapable of breathing free air. The fishes will die in a very short time if we take them out of the water. We even find that there are deep sea fishes, that can only live at a depth of several hundred feet, and if they be drawn out of this depth, near the surface of the water, where the pressure of the water is not so great as they are accustomed to have it, they will die in a very short time. Also we should guard against the mistake of assuming that aquatic creatures are confined to those having physical bodies. The Water Nymphs, the Undines, the Mermen and the Mermaids are all to be taken into consideration when we are discussing the aquatic creatures. None of these can live in any other element save that of water. But even the physical lives that are inhabitants of the water are so innumerable that it staggers the mind to conceive of them. There are thousands of physical lives present in a single drop of water, all of them aquatic creatures that cannot live in any other element. When we come to terrene creatures we find that they are entirely confined to the earth. It is true, the terrene animals breathe the air, and drink water, but the vast majority of them are unable to swim, and those that can do so, only for a very short time, they are unable to propel themselves through the air. They derive their food from the earth, and cannot live any where else. Then we must bear in mind that some of them live in the earth rather than on its surface. Also, we must not forget the Gnomes who are not of a physical constitution, and yet they move in the earth itself, not on its surface. There are many of the Powers that are confined to the earth in this way, even to some of the gods and goddesses, and many of the genii and the daimones. All these are confined to that one element, and have no capacity for any other life. The aery creatures are limited to the air, and cannot live otherwise. It is true that the birds alight upon the earth, both on the surface and in the trees. They derive their food from the earth or near it, and they can to an extent move on the earth, but their real power of locomotion is by wing, which compels them to fly through the air. But, these birds are confined so closely to the earth that they might almost be termed terrene. There are other aery creatures that never touch the earth at all, that live entirely in the air. These include many of the Daimones, Genii, the Sylphs and many other such creatures as well as some of the gods and goddesses. These are confined to the air as the only element in which it is possible for them to live.

We come now to the consideration of the excellence of man over all the other lives. He walks upon the earth, which is his habitation. Through his art he is able to dig down into it to a considerable depth and thus dwell for some time deep under its surface. He can not only swim in the water, but he can build ships in which he can go wherever he wishes on its surface. He can live in them if he so desires. He can construct submarines in which he can travel under water for hours at a time, and can go to the bottom of the sea where the water is not too deep. He has been able to harness the air and compel it to work for him. The water likewise he has made a means of securing power, and the fire likewise is his servant. Water and fire as well as air that are often the means of destruction to the other lives are made to serve the will of man, so that many of his greatest comforts and luxuries are due to the fact that these destructive elements serve him. When man had discovered how to navigate the water with the first rude boat, he had made a tremendous stride in his upward progress. When he discovered fire, and knew how to use it he had taken another great stride. Another epoch in his progress was when he discovered how to smelt the rock in the fire and in this way extract the metals from it and make use of them for his own purposes. The invention of the first wind-mill was the dawn of another epoch of human progress for it was the beginning of man's struggle for the dominion over the air, that it in turn might serve him. Aerial navigation is another triumph of his, but he must regain the power of the ancients to navigate the complete depths of the air, and to be as much at home there as he is upon the earth. We find another great advance step taken when Magnetism was discovered, though unfortunately man has not cultivated this as he should have done, that is not the modern man, he will have to recover the lost arts and sciences of the ancients before he will be in a position to really understand Magnetism. The discovery of Electricity was another great advance step, for in this way has man learned how to harness the lightning, and to make a servant of a force which was up to this time only a destructive power. Next he must go deeper yet, and conquer the Ether as he has the Electricity, then will he enter into a new era of power. For it is the destiny of man to subjugate all of the powers and forces of nature to his will, and cause them to serve his purposes. This power was in the possession of man once, and he must recover it again. However, we must not assume that all of man's power over the elements is to be attained through the practice of the arts and sciences. It is through Occult Discipline that the greatest measure of this power is to be secured. In his Spirit man can travel through the earth, through water, through air and through fire. It is through the ability to project the Spirit from the Body that man attains the fullness of the powers indicated here. Also, he is able through the concentration of his own forces to dominate all of the four elements, this is of course through Magic. In his struggle for supremacy over nature, man has in these degenerate days lost sight of the power of Magic, and

of course it must be restored to the rank of an Exact
Science before he can reach the full measure of his suc-
cess in this work of the subjugation of the elements to
his will. We hear the silly ones speak of this as a
Practical Age, whereas, the thing that dumfounds one is
to see how absolutely impractical the white race is. They
see phenomena and make no effort to understand them,
and learn the Force that produces them, that they may
gain control over that force, and in that way use it for
their own ends. Not less than ten thousand people have
witnessed the phenomenon of Levitation, and not one of
them has ever thought of the problem of harnessing the
Force of Levitation, so as to counter-balance the force
of Gravitation. As a matter of fact, we can harness both
the Forces of Gravitation and Levitation and in this
way make use of them for practical purposes. The only
reason why it has not been done is that the present age
is not a practical age. This knowledge was possessed
and made use of in Ancient Mexico, and there is nothing
to prevent the present generation from doing it. We
have said enough to indicate what can be accomplished
by man in his dealings with the elements. This can be
accomplished both through Applied Science and through
Magic. It is an education in Practical Magic that is
required at this time more than any thing else to enable
man to come into the full realization of his power. The
command to subdue the earth, is as authoritative today
as it ever was. Man must gain control over earth, water,
air and fire. When he is the perfect master of them all,
as well as of all the other departments of Matter, he
will then, and then only, be ready for a higher phase of
life.

But this is not all that man can do. He sees heaven,
and is able to contact it with his senses. The un-men
persists in thinking that heaven can only be realized
through Faith, and a few think that we can through

reason form a conception of it, but none of them realize that it is within our power to render heaven sensible, that is, to contact it through the senses. Heaven is the Soul World, its substance is Psyche, the same substance of which our souls are composed. This being true, the nature of the human soul is identical with the nature of heaven. Heaven is then objective to the soul of man, and being such, all things in heaven are objects of sense to the senses of the soul. It becomes sensible to the senses of the soul as soon as they are opened so that they are able to function in such a way as to make the soul sensible of heaven. The man has not realized his full life until his soul senses are so awakened that he is able to see heaven in the same way that through the action of his physical senses he can see the physical world, heaven must be as objective to his soul, as the physical world is to his body. This is what the awakening of the power of psychic sensation means. The objection to this psychic sensation is that there are so many who confuse the psychic with the astral, but this is not true, the astral is the same as the spiritual, but the psychic is the same as the heavenly, the senses of the soul in fact. When the psychic senses of the soul have been opened, and in this way heaven has been contacted through sense, and all things in heaven have become objective and sensible to the soul through her senses, man will have come to his full realization on the soul plane. But it is not only true that this opening of the soul senses will enable man to become sensible of the action of the soul world, but likewise, he will become receptive to all of the life of heaven, and will take it within himself, and make it a part of himself through this contact. He will in his soul, react to all that is going on in heaven, and will conceive in his soul that which is the image and the likeness of every thing that is in heaven. His soul will become impregnated, and therefore, fecund with all that is in heaven. This is the true meaning of the Heavenly Mar-

riage of the Soul. In this way heaven becomes the
Nuptial Chamber of the soul of man. All of this is within the reach of man. But this is not all, man has it
within the power of his soul to act directly upon heaven,
even to transform it with the action of his soul, to make
use of the senses of his soul as so many active currents
of his own psychic force, and thus to become positive
while heaven itself is negative to him. In other words
he can conquer and subdue heaven itself to his will. He
will never transcend heaven until he has accomplished
this very deed. All that has been indicated here is easily
within the power of man when he has come into full self-
realization of what the Occult life means. This is the
true goal of Initiation. This is why man is called the
Lord of Creation, all of this is literally within his grasp
when he sets in motion all of his powers and forces. Of
course it is the Master-Man alone that can do all of this,
but any man can ultimately become this Master-Man.
Man is the Spouse of God, and she is also the Mistress
of Heaven, of Spirit and of Matter.

But God surroundeth all, and permeateth all, for
He is energy and power; and it is nothing difficult,
my son, to *conceive* God.

All of the Cosmos both the Sensible Cosmos and the
Intelligible Cosmos is completely surrounded by God.
It is completely enclosed by Him, that is by His energy,
and likewise does His energy permeate every particle
of it, so that there is no space between God and anything
else. This is true because God is energy and power. It
is the power of God that moves every thing that is moved,
all motion being the result of the action of this power of
God. It is the energy of God that enters into every
thing, energizes it and makes it live. There is no difficulty for one to *conceive* God. This is true because we
must think of Him as being the totality of energy and
of power. The trouble is that so many try to think of

God as distinct from energy and power, but to conceive of Him we must think of Him as identical with all energy and all power. If we think of God as the totality of energy and power surrounding every thing, and permeating every thing, so that there is no particle not completely surrounded and permeated by this energy and power, and likewise no particle that is not energized and moved by this energy and power, we have conceived God. This is the correct conception of God. At the same time this expression, to *conceive* God, is used in a specific sense. It also means the *conception* of God in the sexual sense. Remember what has been said with reference to the action of God upon the mind of man. God being all energy and power, His energies and powers act upon the mind of man, entering and permeating it through the sense of the mind, so that the mind of the man is completely energized by these energies of God, it is completely moved by the power of God, and the result is, the mind acts in a God-like way, so that it becomes in a sense the reproduction of God, being similar to God in every respect, God being duplicated in the mind of the man. It is thus that God is *conceived* in the mind of man. This *conception* of God in the mind of the man is what gives birth to the God within every one, which is in fact the Image of God present in his mind. This is one effect of the consorting of God with man, of the intercourse between God as husband, and man as wife. It is thus that the image and likeness of God is conceived in the mind of man. Of course this *conception* of God is confined to the mind, it does not extend to any of the other principles. It is thus that through the action of his mind, man may *conceive* and know God. This *conception* of God in the mind is both real and actual. It is a matter of actual experience, and hence, this knowledge of God which a man attains in this way is never erroneous, it is not a matter of opinion, but one of definite knowledge, consciousness, and experience. This is the

God of the Mystic, the Image of God *conceived* and *born* in his own mind. It is thus, that in a sense, the mind of every man may become a *mother* of God, that is to say, the *mother* of the Image of God *conceived* in the mind, and *born* into the reason. Thus is the mind of man the wife of God, and the mother of the Image of God which it *conceives*. Of course, needless to say, this is not experienced by all men, but only by the elect, but it is within the ultimate reach of all. This state is reached only when the human mind becomes a Daimon, for it is only Daimonial Man that is able in this way to recline upon the Nuptial Couch with God, and to *conceive* and give birth to God's Image, as her child. Such men are the true Gnostics and this attainment is a part of the Art of Alchemy.

21. But if thou wouldst Him also *contemplate,* behold the ordering of the Cosmos, and [see] the orderly behaviour of its ordering; behold thou the Necessity of things made manifest, and [see] the Providence of things become and things becoming; behold how Matter is all-full of Life; [behold] this so great God in movement, with all the good and noble [ones] —gods, daimones and men!

Tat. But these are purely energies, O father mine!

Her. If, then, they're purely energies, my son,— by whom, then, are they energized except by God?

Or art thou ignorant, that just as Heaven, Earth, Water, Air, are parts of Cosmos, in just the selfsame way God's parts are Life and Immortality, [and] Energy, and Spirit, and Necessity, and Providence, and Nature, Soul, and Mind, and the Duration of all these that is called Good?

And there is naught of things that have become, or are becoming, in which God is not.

But if thou wouldst Him also *contemplate,* behold

the ordering of the Cosmos, and [see] the orderly
behaviour of its ordering; behold thou the necessity
of things made manifest, and [see] the Providence
of things become and things becoming; behold how
Matter is all-full of Life; [behold] this so great God
in movement, with all the good and noble [ones]—
gods, daimones and men!

While man *conceives* the First God, he *contemplates*
the Second God, Who is in a sense the Cosmos. The
Image of the First God is *conceived* in the mind of man,
by the action of God upon his mind through the energies
and powers of God entering the mind. This being true,
it is the mind of man that *conceives* God, but it is the
reason of the man that *contemplates* the Second God.
This is accomplished by the reason tracing out the
diverse manifestations of the Second God. Let this then
be understood, man *conceives* the First God in his mind,
he *contemplates* the Second God with his reason. In
this process of *contemplation* the reason is first directed
to the ordering of the Cosmos. The Cosmos is the Order
that is manifested by God, it is in fact the mirroring of
God in Matter, using Matter here not in the sense of
physical Matter, but rather in the sense of the Primal
Substance. When the mind has *conceived* God, the reason next directs its attention to this ordering of the
Cosmos, seeing the manner in which God is made manifest in this Order which is the Cosmos. By the ordering
of the Cosmos, we are to understand the mandatory
action of the Thought of God, it is in fact identical with
the Sense-and-Thought of God acting upon Primal Substance and thereby ordering it into the mirroring of this
very same Sense-and-Thought of God. This process the
reason traces out. At the same time it is to be borne
in mind that to do this, the reason must take on this
very ordering, in a word, the reason is ordered in precisely this self same way, so as to become identical with

this Order. Next, the reason must see the orderly
behaviour of this ordering of the Cosmos. This means
the behaviour of the Cosmos in perfect accord with this
ordering. It means that the primal substance of the
Cosmos obeys the ordering of God, so as to perfectly
mirror the Sense-and-Thought of God. To see this the
reason must become this in the perfect sense of the word.
In a word the reason in man must become the perfect
logos of the God Image *conceived* in the mind, and the
exact duplicate of the state of the Cosmos. When the
reason has reached the point of orderly behaviour in
exact harmony with the ordering of Cosmic substance
by the Sense-and-Thought of God, it is ready to take the
next step in the *contemplation* of the Second God. The
next step is to behold the Necessity of things made manifest. Necessity is the determining principle of Cosmos,
that which determines what shall be, and this stage of
contemplation is that act of the reason which enables it
to see the Necessity in action, and likewise, to trace out
the manifestation of this Necessity in the things which
it has determined. This is the process of bearing things,
Cosmos being the sum-total of all things born. It is
the first stage of the creative action of the Cosmos, that
is to say, of the creative activity which brings things
out of Necessity into manifestation. This action of
Necessity bringing things into manifestation is in fact
the action of the Cosmic Logos by which the Ideas of the
things are created. By the reason in man observing
this process, it conforms to the action of Necessity, and
thereby, the Cosmic Ideas of the things, become manifested in the reason as ideas of those things, and these
ideas of the things are identical with the Cosmic Ideas
of the things. In this way is the Cosmic Logos mirrored
in the reason of man. The Providence of things become
and things becoming, is that action of the Cosmos and
of the Logos, by which things are brought into being
from their Ideas. To make this matter clearer, we may

say that the Cosmos is impregnated by the Ideas of things, and as a result, Cosmos conceives their Monads, that is to say, the Monads which are the manifest expression of those Ideas, so that the Ideas have now become Monads. Likewise they are the Monadic states of the things that are to be. When the things have become Monads, these Monads likewise initiate processes of becoming, which are destined to engender things corresponding to them. The action of the reason, when it *contemplates* this Providence of things become and of things becoming, causes its ideas to become monads, of like nature to the Monads engendered or conceived in the Cosmos by the Ideas of the Logos, and also, these Monads initiate the process of becoming things within the human reason. Thus, the entire process of the Providence of things become and things becoming, in this monadic sense, is mirrored in the reason of man. Thus is all that is in the Cosmic Logos perfectly reproduced and duplicated in the reason of the man. The Image of God that was *conceived* in his mind, is in this way *gestated* in his reason so that the reason becomes the womb in which the likeness of the Second God is *gestated* and there prepared for its birth. Thus it will be seen that the function of the reason in man is purely feminine and maternal, just as is that of the mind of man. Just as the mind of man is the Spouse of God and the Mind, so is the reason of man the Spouse of the Cosmic Logos. The next stage in the *Contemplation* of God is when we contemplate how Matter is all-full of Life. The Matter here spoken of is that Primal Substance which gives birth to all things. The reason of man must observe this Matter, and observe how it is all filled full of life, there being no part of it devoid of Life. Life as used here is the Energy which becomes Soul in the plane below. Therefore, it is the Primal Substance permeated and filled with this Life Energy that one is to contemplate. This act of contemplation, has the effect of infusing Life into the Matter of the logos in man, so that it takes on the condition of the Cosmic Matter which is all-full of life. In this way, man can contemplate all of these aspects of the Cosmos synthesized as one Cosmos, thus the Second God, in all of His movements. By such act of *contemplation*, man is able to bring into his reason all of this Cosmos, so that the Second God is positively *gestated* in his reason. With the Cosmos, he must synthesize all the good and noble ones, Gods, daimones and men. He must see them all as united in Cosmos, as each and every one having his Monad forever fixed in Cosmos. Thus is the unity of all established in his reason. Not only does he in this way understand the unity of all, but his *contemplation* fixes that unity in himself. In his reason are now forever fixed the ideas and the monads of all of the good and noble ones, the gods, daimones and men of the entire Cosmos and Universe, of all time, past, present and to come. They are all synthesized in him, so that all are within him. By this act of contemplation, he takes on the entire Cosmos, and becomes it. In this way, all that has been imaged in his reason is mirrored in his soul. Just as the Unity of the Second God is mirrored in the reason, so is His diversity in the different good and noble ones, gods, daimones and men, mirrored in his soul. Thus the images of all the good and noble ones, all the gods, all the daimones and all men, are born in the soul of the man who has learned to *contemplate* God. Through this birth into the soul, she becomes fecund with the energies of all the good and noble ones, the gods, daimones and the men. It is in this way that we *contemplate* God with the reason, but *conceive* Him with the mind.

Tat. But these are purely energies, O father mine!

Tat conceives all these things to be purely energies, and he finds great difficulty in contemplating an energy, and also, he is unable to see how God can be seen in pure

energies. Evidently, he is still troubled with the idea
of a Personal God, and is unable to see how God can be
seen in a number of energies. We find the same difficulty in the minds of people of the present day. They
cannot see God through the contemplation of the energies
present in Matter, they think that they must form a
concept of God through the contemplation of personal
and even human characteristics. They will take certain
human characteristics of a psychic nature, and reduce
them to abstractions, and synthesize them into an homo-
geneous entity and call it God. These people will take
Love, Mercy, Justice, Truth, Compassion, Purity and
similar Moral Virtues in men, and will reduce them to
Abstract Principles and then they will say that these
Abstract Moral Principles collectively constitute God.
To tell them that these moral virtues do not exist as
Abstract Principles will dumfound these people, and yet
such is the case. If we say that Justice is not a characteristic of God, we will shock all of the feelings of these
people, and yet the fact is that Justice is not an attribute
of God. Justice is not an Absolute but a Relative Virtue.
It depends upon the relationship subsisting between two
or more people, each of whom possesses rights which the
others are bound to respect, were it not for this very
condition, there would be no such thing as Justice. Now,
no one has a single right, so far as God is concerned. All
that any one has, God has given to him, therefore God
owes him nothing, while he owes every thing to God; but
that which God has given you, is not yours as a matter
of right, but yours as a matter of His favour, and only
so long as His favour shall continue. This being true,
you have no rights at all so far as God is concerned,
therefore, nothing that He can do will be unjust, and at
the same time nothing that He can do will be just, seeing
that it is not conceding your rights, but rather giving
you something that you have no right to. God is, therefore, neither just or unjust, Justice is a Moral Virtue

entirely foreign to the Essence of God. Justice belongs
to the relations of particularized life, but is no part of
the life of the Absolute, hence, we cannot see God in an
abstraction of Justice. Love, Mercy and Compassion,
each involve the relation of Subject and Object, and this
is a relation that does not exist or rather subsist with
God. He is the only one, and is conscious of nothing
but Himself. It will be seen from this that we cannot
see God through the contemplation of any abstraction of
the moral virtues of the personal life. We can see Him
only through the contemplation of the Energies which
are set in motion by Him. We can know God only as the
Energizer of His energies, and thus through an understanding of the essence and nature of the energies, we
will be able to reach an understanding of the Energizer
of those energies, through a knowledge of that which He
energizes. This is another way of saying that we know
the Workman by a study of his workmanship, and the
character of the Actor by his action. The great value
of this Sermon to Tat is, that he was in the same stage
of development and of consciousness as are the Mystics
and the Metaphysicians of the present day, and that he
asked the same fool questions, and advanced the same
fool arguments, and cherished the same fool notions then
that they do now, therefore, the arguments of Hermes
apply in the same degree to the fool doctrines of the most
Progressive of the Advanced Thought of the present
day. As the wisdom of Hermes was superior to that of
Tat, so is the wisdom of Hermetic Philosophy superior
to the most advanced of the Advanced Thought of the
present day.

Her. If, then, they're purely energies, my son,—
by whom, then, are they energized except by God?

Hermes brings out the point that all energies must be
energized by something else, and if all these are purely
energies, then they must be energized by something apart

from themselves. Now, there can be nothing back of these energies save God, hence God alone can be the Energizer of these energies. As this is obviously true, a study of these energies is a study of the energizing of God, and hence a study of the activity of God, therefore, it is a study of God Himself. This demonstration shows how we can with perfect accuracy reach an understanding of God Himself.

Or art thou ignorant, that just as Heaven, Earth, Water, Air, are parts of Cosmos, in just the selfsame way God's parts are Life and Immortality, [and] Energy, and Spirit, and Necessity, and Providence, and Nature, Soul, and Mind, and the Duration of all these that is called Good?

Cosmos as a whole we have indicated as the Order mirrored in Matter by God. The parts of Cosmos are Heaven and the Elements from which all things are made. In like manner, God is one, and yet, the parts of God we can easily name. This does not mean that we can separate these and thus eliminate God. On the contrary, these parts are not added together to make God, rather do they all grow out of God. They are the parts manifested, the manifestations of God, and they go to make up God Manifest. These parts of God are Life and Immortality, by which we are to understand the Live Principle which is the engenderer of Soul, as well as that which perpetuates Life without end. Energy, or the Essence that entering into all things, energizes them, and makes them move, the essence that gives action to all things. Spirit, or the Principle between Physical Matter and Soul. Necessity, or that which determines the Ideas of all things. Providence, or that which causes the Ideas of all things to bring forth the Monads corresponding to them, thus the Monads of all things. Nature, or the process of being born in all things, the perpetual coming

into being of all things. Soul and Mind, and Duration
which is Eternity or Æon are also parts of God. By
contemplating all these as parts of God, not as something
distinct from Him, but as in Him, as so many aspects of
His Being, we will be able to see what God is, because
we will see Him as the Unity manifesting in all these
aspects and manifestation. But the great value of this
aspect of our *contemplation* will be that we will not only
bring about the perfection of Mind in our mind, of
Necessity and Providence in our reason, as well as the
filling of our Matter, that is the Primal Substance of
our logos, with Life, but we will also surcharge it with
Immortality, so that as a result of this *contemplation* or
reason will become immortal in itself. But this is not
all, Energy will be drawn into the soul, so that it will be
energized by the Energy of God, and Nature as the one
process of being brought to birth will be mirrored in the
soul, so that this One Nature will become the *nature* of
our soul, giving her a Cosmic nature instead of an individual nature. The *contemplation* of God as Soul will
cause this Soul to be mirrored in our soul so that she
will become identical with the One Soul. By *contemplating* God as Duration or Æon we will establish this as
our nature and our life, and in this way, by having
Eternity mirrored in us, do we attain Eternal Life thus
does our soul become Eternal and not simply Immortal.
By *contemplating* God as Spirit, our own spirit is so
transmuted as to become the Image of God as Spirit. In
this way is the Image of God born in our mind, reason,
soul and spirit, and only our body remains human, all
else has become divine. It is this *contemplation* of God
that makes man himself Divine and no longer human.
Thus do we see the value of this *contemplation* of God.
This of course is the exercise of the Art of Divine
Alchemy.

And there is naught of things that have become, or are becoming, in which God is not.

In this statement, Hermes informs us that God is in every thing that has become, that He is in all the things that now are, or that ever have been, and likewise He is in all the things that are now in process of coming into being, and of course He will likewise be in all the things that ever shall come into being. In other words, the entire creative process is in reality the process of God giving birth to all things, and as He or rather She, can only bear from within Herself, all that is, that was and that ever shall be, is born out of God, therefore, is of the Essence of God, hence Divine. God, that is to say, the Energy and the Essence of God, is present in all things. This being true, God is in this way present in us, in every part of us, and what we must learn to do, is to permit the manifestation in action of this God Principle in us, this Energy of God, so that we may be energized by it, and may in this way come to the full manifestation of this Divinity that is inherently present in us. In other words, this Latent Divine Energy that is in us must become Kinetic Divine Energy, our Latent Divinity must be aroused into Kinetic Divine Energy. Thus will we became truly and esentially divine. This is the true purpose and the invariable result of this *contemplation* of God. It is in this way that our *nature* is transmuted from the human to the Divine, and this is the true Art of Alchemy, the transmutation of humanity into Divinity, both in life and in *nature*.

LESSON X.

GOD AND MATTER.

22. *Tat.* Is He in Matter, father, then?

Her. Matter, my son, is separate from God, in order that thou may'st attribute unto it the quality of space. But what thing else than mass think'st thou it is, if it's not energized? Whereas if it be energized, by whom is it made so? For energies, we said, are parts of God.

By whom are, then, all lives enlivened? By whom are things immortal made immortal? By whom changed things made changeable?

And whether thou dost speak of Matter, or of Body, or of Essence, know that these too are energies of God; and that materiality is Matter's energy, that corporality is Bodies' energy, and that essentiality doth constitute the energy of Essence; and this is God—the All.

Tat. Is He in Matter, father, then?

After hearing the logos expounded which indicates that God is in every thing, Tat is interested to know if this imminence of God extends to Matter as well. He has learned that God is in every thing else, there being nothing but Matter left in which God could enter beyond what he has already been told, God is in, therefore, he wishes to know if God is in Matter as well. It should be borne in mind that the Matter spoken of here is not the Primal Substance of things, it is Physical Matter, all below the Plane of Spirit. The question is, is God present

(183)

in Physical Matter? Bear in mind that this is the Second
or Manifest God rather than the First or Unmanifest God
that he is speaking of.

Her. Matter, my son, is separate from God, in order that thou may'st attribute unto it the quality of
space. But what thing else than mass think'st thou
it is, if it's not energized? Whereas if it be energized, by whom is it made so? For energies, we said,
are parts of God.

Matter is separted from God in the sense that Matter
possesses the quality of space. Matter is therefore stuff,
that is, it is space-filling. It is this which differentiates
Matter from God, Matter is space-filling, and its operations are determined by space. A material body must
pass from one point in space to another, thus moving
through space, and at different times being confined to
different points in space. God, on the other hand, is present equally in all parts of space, hence, so far as God is
concerned there is no such thing as space. As God is
Omni-present He does not move in space, and is not
extended through space, we cannot measure the extension of God, therefore, being every where present as
Energy, God does not possess the quality of space. This
then is what distinguishes Matter from God. In this
sense, Matter is distinct from God, and hence we cannot
include Matter in the Second God. At the same time,
if Matter were not energized, it would be nothing but
mass. That would be its only quality. However, we
know that Matter, is moved, for the quality of all material bodies is in the fact that they are moved through
space. Were it not that all material bodies were moved
through space, Matter would not have, the quality of
space, this quality being given to it by reason of the
movement of all material bodies, and, if Matter had no
other quality save that of mass, no material body could

move, and in that case it would not be Matter at all. Matter is Matter because it is moved, and all movement is the result of energy acting upon mass, therefore, Matter is Matter because it is energized. It is the passibility of Matter to the passion of energy that constitutes it Matter. This being the case, there is no such thing as Matter apart from energy. It could not for one instant exist were it separated from energy, its very existence depends upon its being in a perpetual state of being energized. Matter must at all times be energized in order that it may *be,* then the question is, whence come the energies, and by whom is it energized. It can only be energized by reason of the action of energies upon it, and all the energies are parts of God, hence, God is the energizer of Matter, and it is His energies, which are all parts of Him, that energize Matter. In a sense then, God is the husband who is in a perpetual state of coetus with Matter which is His spouse. His energies are the sexual energies, containing the Spermal Seed, which enter into Matter as the Matrix and impregnate and fecundate it with the spermal seed of God coming through the energizing of Matter by these energies that are parts of God, ever subsisting in Him. Matter being receptive to God, becomes the receptacle for all of the energies of God, and is thereby the Vessel in which the energies of God center, and into which they all flow. Thus we may say that Matter is separated from God in the sense of being the receptacle of His energies, and the Matrix into which His Seed are dropped. Matter is separated from God in the sense of Being the receptacle for all of the energies of God.

By whom are, then, all lives enlivened? By whom are things immortal made immortal? By whom changed things made changeable?

All lives are enlivened, that is are endowed with life,

by reason of the action of Life upon Matter. It should be borne in mind that life is never an attribute of matter. Material bodies do not live in the sense of possessing life as a part of themselves, life has entered into them, and they live because of the action upon their tissues of this life that is temporarily tabernacling within them, were it not for the life that is energizing them, they would be dead bodies. Lives in the sense of living things, are enlivened or made to live, by reason of the life that is energizing them, and this life is the result of Life acting upon them, and Life is an energy of God, a part of God in fact, hence it is God who sends His Life into all living things and makes them live. It is in the same way that immortal things get their immortality. It is not an attribute of their own nature, but is the result of that Immortality which is a part of God, entering into them, so that they, being energized by God's Immortality, become immortal, by reason of their being energized by that immortality. It is the same way with the changes that are to be seen in all changed things. They are changed, and rendered changeable, that is, capable of being changed, by reason of the action of energy upon them. They are the moved, and they are moved by reason of the energy that moves them. All changes and transformations are the work of energy, energizing bodies, and as all energies are parts of God, it is God who changes all things that are changeable, in fact their changeability is the result of their being energized by God through the action of His energies upon them.

And whether thou dost speak of Matter, or of Body, or of Essence, know that these too are energies of God; and that materiality is Matter's energy, that corporality is Bodies' energy, and that essentiality doth constitute the energy of Essence; and this is God—the All.

Not only is all that we have stated true, but even Matter, Body and Essence are themselves energies of God. This is, of course, hard for one to understand at first, but nevertheless it is true. The energy of Matter is materiality. Notice that Matter here is distinguished from Corporality or Body, and hence we are to understand Body as referring to Organic Matter in the sense of all Matter that is organized into bodies, while Matter is used here with reference to Inorganic Matter, Matter in a state of diffusion, free Matter so to speak. We are informed that the energy of Matter is materiality. The energy of Matter is that which constitutes it Matter. Materiality is therefore, that form of action which differentiates Matter from all else. It is an energizing of Matter that causes it to be material, that is, that determines its identity as Matter. To understand this, we must bear in mind that all Substance is derived from the Primal Substance, and is in fact a differentiation of that Primal Substance. Materiality as the energy of Matter, is that particular form of energy, the action of which transmutes the Primal Substance into Matter. It is the energy, the effect of which is to establish a state of stability, and inertia in whatever it energizes. The inertia of Matter is due to substance being energized with this energy of materiality. This is the energy and the quality of diffused Matter. We come now to Organic or Corporal Matter, the Matter, present in Bodies. The energy of Bodies is corporality. By corporality we are to understand that which constitutes any thing corporal. We are informed that this is an energy, and the meaning of this statement is that when Matter is not only energized by the energy of materiality, but also by the energy of corporality, such Matter is organized into a corporal body. Corporality is, therefore, the body-forming energy. It is this energy that constructs bodies from the Matter which it energizes. Essentiality is the energy that renders that which is energized by it, Essence. We will have to see what we mean by Essence, in order that we may reach an understanding of the meaning of essentiality. Esse is the Verb to Be. It is the Esse of any thing that makes it what it is, that causes it to *be,* and this is similar to Beness. Essence is the activity which results from Esse, Being as distinguished from Beness. Essentiality is an energy that is of the quality of Esse, which acting upon Substance, causes it to conform in action to the *Norm* in Esse, and thus become the manifestation of Esse, due to the fact that it is energized by the energy of Esse, which is the essentiality. Thus, substance energized by the essential energy of Esse becomes Essence. For this reason we can see that essentiality, corporality, and materiality are all of them energies, and that it is their energizing of Substance that causes the appearance of Essence, Body and Matter. All energies are parts of God, are His activities, therefore, all this is the act of God. God as the First God is the Source of all energies, and as the Second God He is the totality of all energies, hence, God is the Principia of all things, even Matter and all Bodies. Matter is in this sense the Form of God, a Form that is produced by the energizing of the energies of God.

23. And in the All is naught that is not God. Wherefore nor size, nor space, nor quality, nor form, nor time, surroundeth God; for He is All, and All surroundeth all, and permeateth all.

Unto this Reason (*Logos*), son, thy adoration and thy worship pay. There is one way alone to worship God; [it is] not to be bad.

And in the All is naught that is not God. Wherefore nor size, nor space, nor quality, nor form, nor time, surroundeth God; for He is All, and All surroundeth all, and permeateth all.

The All here alluded to, is that Unity made up of the totality of all things, but viewed as an Unity. In this Unity of All there is nothing that is not God, for all things are the product of energizing on the part of the diverse energies, all of which subsist in God. This being true, in the All there is nothing but God. God is, therefore, not surrounded by either size, space, quality, form or time. God is not separate from any of these; that He may be surrounded by them, but rather are they all manifestations of God, and are to be found in God, not apart from Him, or surrounding Him. Size is determined by the extension of a body, and this is through the corporality of the energizing of its Matter, and hence, size is the product of energizing on the part of energy, which is a part of God, hence, it is God who gives to all things their size; therefore, all sizes subsist in God. Space we have seen is the product of God for it is the expanse through which all bodies move, and as they move by reason of energy, space is nothing other than the path pursued by energy, which is a part of God, therefore, all space is in God. Quality is determined by the energy that is energizing a thing, and hence it is determined by God, and subsists in God. For it is the product of the energizing of Matter by energy, and as energy is in God, so is all form in God and not apart from Him. Time is the Periodicity of motion, and as all motion is the result of energizing and is the act of energy, it follows that time is determined by the energies which are parts of God, hence all time subsists in God and never separate from Him. For this reason all these are contained in God, none of them are separate from Him as being something outside of Him, therefore they do not surround Him, but are contained within Him. God is the All, which itself surroundeth all things, containing all within itself, and giving birth to all, as well as supporting all things. This Unity of All which is God permeateth all things, and energizes them, for they are all of them, merely so many forms of His energy, so many acts of His energizing.

Unto this Reason (*Logos*), son, thy adoration and thy worship pay. There is one way alone to worship God; [it is] not to be bad.

Having finished the instruction, Hermes now urges Tat to pay his adoration and worship to the Reason which he has learned. This instruction is stated to be the revelation of the Logos, and hence it must be grasped by the reason of the student. This knowledge is, therefore, not something merely to be studied, but something to be adored and worshipped. By worship we are to understand that reverence for something above our reach, something that we have not attained unto, and by adoration we are to understand the striving to lose ourselves in the object of our adoration. Therefore, one must look upon this teaching as being something beyond the grasp of the reason, and yet he should lose his reason in the contemplation of the teaching. In a word, one should not try to master this teaching, but rather he should strive to completely yield himself up to the teaching, that his whole being may be transmuted by it, and thereby he may become the knowledge that is given in this logos. There is but one way to worship God and that is to refrain from being bad. In other sermons, we are told that Matter is the proper place of bad, and that the Good cannot dwell in Matter, therefore, the instruction not to be bad, means to have all of our conduct determined by the mind and the reason, and never to yield ourselves to the influence either of the senses or of our *nature*. This is the way to worship God, by controlling the soul, spirit and the body by the mind and reason, to let the Good express itself through all of our actions, thus redeeming our life from the influence of our *nature* and likewise from the psychological reactions to the energizing through the senses. Cease to image in the soul the objects of sense, and learn to image the thoughts of the mind and the ideas of the reason. This is the way to transmute the soul after the image and likeness of God, and it is in this way that we cease to be bad, and become Good. This is the only way to worship God, by becoming like Him, in the way that has been indicated in the earlier part of this Treatise. Man becomes Good through the transmutation of his soul into the image of God through the exercise of his mind and reason to the point of entirely dominating all of the psychic activity of the soul. This is the Art of Alchemy that will elevate the soul of man into the status of Divinity, this is the one and only Path which will lead the aspiring soul to God-hood.

THE END.

THE END.

CPSIA information can be obtained
at www.ICGtesting.com
Printed in the USA
BVHW041756210121
598348BV00011B/130

9 781497 977860